Antique Garden Tools
& Accessories

Myra Yellin Outwater

Photography by Eric Boe Outwater

4880 Lower Valley Road, Atglen, PA 19310 USA

Designed by Bonnie M. Hensley
Cover design by Bruce M. Waters
Type set in Zurich BdXCn BT/ZapfChan Dm BT

ISBN: 0-7643-1478-5
Printed in China
1 2 3 4

Published by Schiffer Publishing Ltd.
4880 Lower Valley Road
Atglen, PA 19310
Phone: (610) 593-1777; Fax: (610) 593-2002
E-mail: Schifferbk@aol.com
Please visit our web site catalog at www.schifferbooks.com
We are always looking for people to write books on new and related subjects. If you have an idea for a book please contact us at the above address.

This book may be purchased from the publisher.
Include $3.95 for shipping.
Please try your bookstore first.
You may write for a free catalog.

In Europe, Schiffer books are distributed by
Bushwood Books
6 Marksbury Ave.
Kew Gardens
Surrey TW9 4JF England
Phone: 44 (0) 20 8392-8585; Fax: 44 (0) 20 8392-9876
E-mail: Bushwd@aol.com
Free postage in the U.K., Europe; air mail at cost.

Contents

Acknowledgments

Our deepest gratitude to Philip Norman, Assistant Curator of the Museum of Garden History in London. His unfailing kindness, enthusiasm, and knowledge of garden tools have enhanced our book.

Victoria Farrow, director of the Museum of Garden History

Monika Dorman

Lynn Chase and Anne Rowe for allowing us to photograph their collections

Jim Hinck

Thank you to:

Peter Goldfarb	Eli Leon	Jan Johnson
Roberta BenDavid	Jan Hinson	Marge and Gerald Gayner
Gramercy Tavern	Tom Beck	Mary Taylor

Photo by Monika Dorman.

For more than three hundred years, gardening has been one of the most popular hobbies.

Form and Function

Creativity and Ingenuity

Photo by Monika Dorman.

Without tools, man could not garden. Since prehistoric times, man has made implements from animal bones, tree limbs, and stones to create "extra hands" to help him in his daily chores, but nowhere is this more apparent than in the garden, where for centuries man has created "finger-like" implements to dig, plant, aerate, cut and plow fields. And as tool manufacture became more advanced, man used other materials such as iron, wood and cast metal for his tools. At the same time gardeners copied general tools, adopting them to specific garden functions. Today tools are made from such diverse substances as iron, steel, aluminum, galvanized metal, glass and plastic.

But what makes these garden tools unique is the fact that their design has evolved from functional needs, and the results have not only been inge-nious, but artful. Nineteenth century English garden tool catalogs list hundreds of task specific tools. Gardeners eagerly ordered dibbers, mattocks, potato hoes, onion hoes, daisy grubbers, weed hoes, torpedo hoes, spud hoes, half-moon shaped hoes, swan-necked hoes, short-handled hoes, long-handled hoes, claws, weeders, forcers, straighteners, garden reels, rakes, turfing irons, watering cans, water tanks, lawn mowers, lawn rollers, weed whackers and slashers.

This book looks back at two hundred years of garden history, and attempts to not only identify the tools but specify their functions. As man became more sophisticated he was no longer content to have just one tool for each chore, and soon a variety of tools developed with specific needs as to gardening tasks and garden sites.

The most essential qualities of a garden tool, other than function, are durability and portability. Working tools had to be well made to survive weather and hard labor. They also had to be light enough to be carried into the field.

The earliest known garden tools were "slashers," "cutters," and "grafters." By the seventeenth and eighteenth centuries there were choppers, saws, and shears. By the nineteenth century, gardeners were demanding specifically shaped handles and angled blades. It was common to find tools with blade-ends that were triangular, swan-necked, crick-shaped, heart-shaped, open, closed, and rolled.

Hoes are another example of functional diversity. There were spud hoes for digging weeds, potato hoes for digging potatoes, onion hoes for cultivating onions, clay hoes for working in clay soils, Dutch hoes and torpedo hoes for difficult stone-imbedded fields, daisy grubbers for weeding daisies, mattocks for weeds, asparagus knives, beetroot knives, and moss scrapers.

By the twentieth century there were tools that served dual purposes, such as multi-purpose rake/spades, walking stick tools/saws, canes with handles that doubled as weeders or slashers, and combo walking stick/fruit pickers. In addition tool sets were sized for women, senior gardeners, thin or hefty hands. Many companies manufactured tools for children to stimulate an early interest in gardening and botany.

Practical gardeners also bought gardening kits—long handled poles that came with an assortment of attachments such as rake heads, spade blades, prongs, and mattocks.

Gardeners have always appreciated nice looking tools. Some antique tools have engraved brass or gold initials on their handles. Others have carved intricate designs. Others, like this 1940s-1950s American trio of hand fork, hand shovel, and claw make an attractive set with their red and green trim. Alone these tools now are worth about $25-35 apiece. But with their original box shown below, the set is worth between $80-95.

Ordinary household tools inspired garden tools. It is easy to see the relationship of grass shears and pruning knives to household scissors and knives. Hand weeders and cultivators are similar in form to simple household forks. Spades can be traced to spoons and ordinary levers, and it is a simple jump to see the connection between pots and water pitchers to watering cans.

In 1927 Sheffield toolmaker, C.T. Skelton was making thirty-five different kinds of spades, with different finishes and sizes, and differently styled handles—plain, turned wood, "D" and "T" shaped handles. The company also made thirty-five different forks for asparagus, beetroot, and potatoes, as well as tools with characteristics specific to the regional styles of Cheshire, Guernsey, Irish, Kentish, and Scotch.

This book concentrates mainly on antique garden tools of French, English and American manufacture. We do not list German, Italian, Spanish or Dutch tools because we did not find any in our research. We can assume however that their tools must have developed along parallel lines with the ones shown in this book because the English were large-scale manufacturers and exported tools world wide throughout what was then the British Empire.

Without tools man could not garden. *Courtesy of Larkspur Farms.*

A page from a 1909 William Wood & Son mail order catalog. These catalogs are valued at $35-50 depending on their illustrations. English. *Courtesy of the Museum of Garden History.*

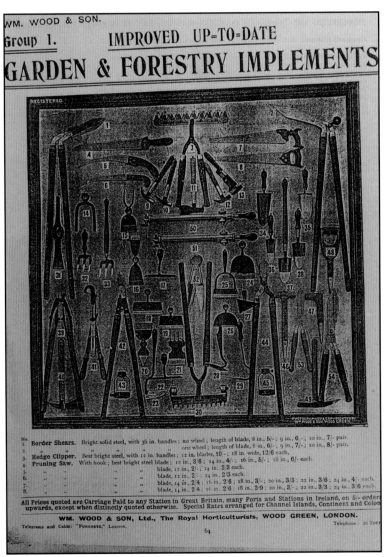

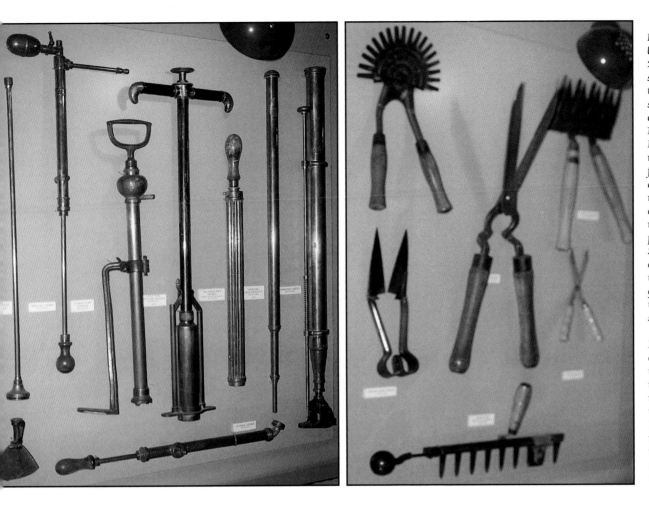

Left: Tools of the late 19th and early 20th century began to show a new technology. These sprayers are from the collection of the Museum of Garden History and were mostly used to spray for pest and plant diseases such as mildew. Chemicals and powders were mixed with water to provide the "cure." Sometimes a white-out powder was used to spray the glass in greenhouses to shade the plants from strong summer sun.

Right: These multi-cut English hedge trimmers are a bridge into a new age of tool mechanization. By the late 1940s and 1950s, these will be replaced by electric trimmers. *Courtesy of the Museum of Garden History.*

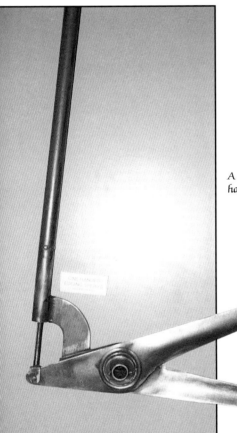

A 20th century English long-handled lawn edger.

An upright Follows & Bates, c. 1885, lawn mower with 6-inch cylinder blades and wooden grass catching box. *Courtesy of the Museum of Garden History.*

Very early tools of Roman origin have been discovered in archeological digs in England. Most of these have been associated with viniculture. Various brass pots and watering containers have been noted presumably of Dutch origin, and one must assume that the Dutch hoe must have come from Holland.

Beauty in Everyday Life

The wealthy have always prized beauty especially in their household objects, but what is most appealing about ordinary garden tools is that even the working class took pride in their tools' design and decorated them and inscribed their initials on their handles. The nineteenth century heart-shaped turfing iron is a perfect example of how an object with such a lowly function can have such intrinsic beauty.

Eighteenth century toolmakers created personalized brass and silver detailing. Towards the end of the nineteenth century manufacturers were briskly selling red, blue, green and yellow painted watering cans, hand-forks, hand-spades, and hoes. Nineteenth century advertised "japanned red" watering cans, "japanned black" garden hoes, and "bright and blue" fork-end and double-head hoes." The ultimate in garden tool design is English sculptor Tony Cragg's 1999 design for the Tate Modern Museum in London of a sculptural set of garden tools—a white, plastic hand fork and trowel created in the shape of a cactus

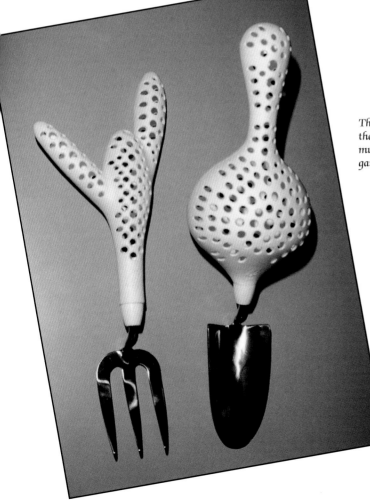

These garden tools were designed by sculptor Tony Cragg in 1999 for the Tate Modern Museum in London as a joint project between the museum and Homebase in an attempt to produce aesthetic, sculpted garden and home objects. $75.

1

Botanists, Plant Seekers, Gentlemen

When we look at the history of gardening, it is important to note that there have always been several kinds of gardeners—botanists, home gardeners, gentlemen gardeners, and ordinary workers. By the eighteenth century, gardens were no longer basic necessities, but an adornment to homes and a symbol of wealth. By the nineteenth century, educated gardeners had developed such an interest in botany and specimen hunting that there were hundreds of how-to books about developing new varieties and hybrids of existing flowers. By the end of the century, there was a new class of gardener, the scientific and amateur botanist. Specimen gardeners resulted in the creation of natural history museums and private showplace gardens. Among the first in England were the Royal Botanical Gardens at Kew, in 1841.

Specimen Carriers

Bulb collecting is not a new concept. Plant hunters were recorded as early as 1495 BC when Queen Hatshepsut sent an expedition to Somalia to bring back an incense tree to Egypt. European, Chinese, and Far Eastern plant collectors sought new species for food and medicine. In England, John Tradescant the Elder and his son, John, are generally thought to be the most celebrated English plant hunters of the seventeenth century. They were gardeners to Charles I and II and introduced flowers, shrubs and trees from Africa, Europe, Russia, and North America to England.

In 1637 a mania for rare tulip bulbs, Tulipomania, almost precipitated a financial depression in Dutch society at the time. By the seventeenth century, horticultural experimenting created so many new species of tulips and bulbs were so coveted that they became a commodity. One of the most famous was a tulip bulb named *"Semper augustus."*

By the early nineteenth century, one of the most popular hobbies of the European upper classes was botanical specimen collecting, and their new heroes were specimen and plant hunters.

By the mid-nineteenth century, European gardeners were growing such exotic specimens as Himalayan rhododendrons, azaleas, camellias and gardenias. One of the best-known plant seekers was Joseph Hooker whose father, William was named the first director of the Royal Botanic Gardens at Kew in 1841. Joseph Hooker, who became the second director of Kew Gardens in 1865, traveled to the Himalayas to bring back exotic speci-

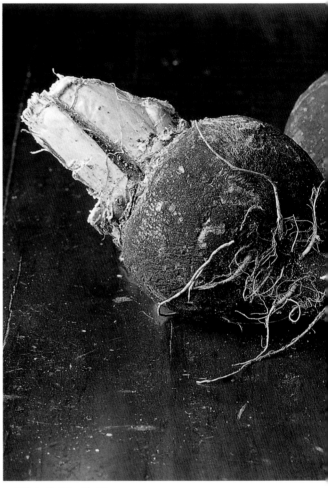

Photo by Monika Dorman.

Hobbyists, Food and Flower Fanciers

mens of flowers and plants. It was Hooker who introduced rhododendrons to England and made growing hybrid rhododendrons fashionable among the English. Hooker's writings and drawings are still studied by students of garden history.

Reginald Farrar was another well-known plant seeker. His 1911 book "Among the Hills: A book of Joy in High Places" describes his adventures in the Alps searching for alpine plants.

One of the earliest flower fads was the carnation which was introduced in the seventeenth century. In 1629 English gardener, John Parkinson wrote that there were 50 different "cultivars" or hybrids. In 1689 an anonymous French writer wrote a manual for amateur "jardinier fleurists" on how to raise and cultivate the flower and what were the best varieties. "Pinks" or "dianthus" became such a craze in the early nineteenth century that soon there were hundreds of cultivars. Dahlias were introduced to Europe in 1804. By 1830 there were over 1,500 varieties, making it the most popular flower of the day. Pansies became popular in the 1830s. Camellias were so popular by the early nineteenth century that the fashionable built camellia houses for the flowers. The popularity of glass houses or greenhouses coincides with the fact that the tax on sheet glass was abolished in the early nineteenth century. One of the most ardent camellia fanciers was Queen Victoria who began to grow camellias on Osbourne House on the Isle of Wight in the 1840s.

Queen Victoria was only one of many members of the English royalty devoted to her garden. Princess Augusta (1719-1772) the wife of Frederick, Prince of Wales created a nine acre botanical garden that became the origins of the Royal Botanic Gardens at Kew. Queen Adelaide, (1792-1849) the wife of William VI was also a keen gardener. She landscaped the royal gardens and was a patroness of the Metropolitan Society of Florists and Amateurs.

Victorian garden writers John and Jane Loudon introduced the concept of carpet bedding in the 1870s and one of the best flowers for this purpose was the verbena, a new variety introduced in 1879 by English garden writer Henry Eckford. In 1882 Eckford also developed the first modern Sweet Pea, Bronze William, in his nursery in Wem, Shropshire.

Climbing roses were introduced from America in the late 1800s and soon gardeners were building pergolas. Large flowered clematis was another popular climbing flower.

By the end of the nineteenth century there were many professional plant hunters and plant hunting expeditions. The Royal Botanic Gardens at Kew and the Royal Horticultural Society sponsored expeditions. Commercial nurseries, also hired plant hunters and sponsored expeditions. Business was flourishing and everyone was trying to develop new hybrids for the voracious tastes of gardeners.

A vasculum was a small portable metal carrying case used by botanists and plant seekers to bring back botanical specimens, seedlings and plants. These cases got their name from the Latin word meaning "small vessel." The word also refers to the wood/glass sectioned containers. A vasculum in good condition is valued in the range of $100-$250 depending on condition. Rust, dents and missing pieces of glass detract from the value.

Royal Doulton plant specimen jug (the handle and metal lid are missing), 19th century, English. This jug, which depicts a plant hunter with his vasculum examining a plant specimen, was made at Doulton's Burslem factory in Stoke-on-Trent, England, in the early 1880s. Vasculum was a 19th century word taken from the Latin meaning "little vessel," used to describe the small portable metal cases carried by botanists into the field to bring back botanical specimens and young plants. Courtesy of the Museum of Garden History.

19th century aluminum carrying case or vasculum. Courtesy of the Museum of Garden History.

French, c. 1880, $125-150. This vasculum or specimen carrying case was in use in France, the United States, and England during the late 19th and early 20th centuries. Courtesy of Riverbank Antiques.

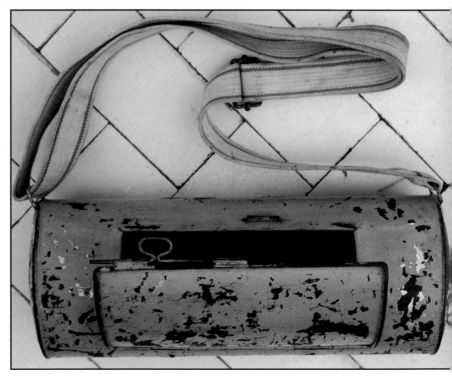

Vasculum, English, 19th century.
Courtesy of Riverbank Antiques.

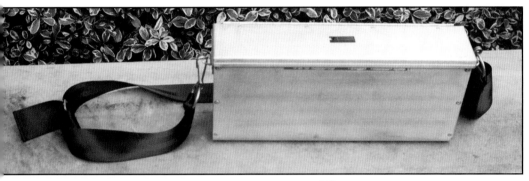

Vasculum, 1990s, English, aluminum.
Courtesy of the Museum of Garden History.

Terrarium or specimen carrying case, English, c. 1900, $100-250. This is a small greenhouse version of a specimen carrying case. Glass domed tops and sloping sides not only protected the plants and increased visibility, but also maximized exposure to sun. This version was often used to carry fern seedlings. It would be worth more if the glass were intact. *Courtesy of Riverbank Antiques.*

An early 20th century drawing. *Courtesy of Riverbank Antiques.*

15

Another version of a square, specimen carrying case. *Courtesy of Riverbank Antiques.*

Miniature terracotta greenhouse and carrying case, English, c. 1950, $40-75. This small, compact case was designed to carry seedlings. *Courtesy of The Sugarplum.*

Holland bulb racks, 1940s, $15- 25 each. *Courtesy of The Sugarplum.*

British, 1860s, $50-65. Mrs. Isabella Mary Beeton, (1836-65) was a popular authority on home management. She and her husband Sidney co-authored many books. Their books were well marketed. Sidney Beeton wrote the Beeton book of Garden Management, which was first published in the early 1860s as Every Day Gardening. It was later revised and expanded and became a classic book for more than thirty years. The last revision was in the 1890s. Nineteenth century gardening books were noteworthy for their elaborate bindings and cover designs with stylized flowers, intertwined vines and plantings. Vintage gardening books range in value from $50-100. Courtesy of Riverbank Antiques.

Courtesy of The Sugarplum.

Garden Books

We have included garden books and gardening magazines in this chapter because, since the 1700s, garden books have been essential to gardeners teaching them gardening methods, showing them the kinds of tools available, and providing instruction as to how to make them.

Flower gardening as we know it today is a relatively new idea. It wasn't until the early nineteenth century when the middle classes, as well as the nobility and wealthy, had the luxury and opportunity to grow flowers. Englishman John Loudon and his wife Jane are generally considered the instigators of the new gardening popularity. They founded *The Gardeners' Magazine*, a nineteenth century periodical that became immensely popular. Later Loudon wrote and published *The Suburban Gardener and Villa Companion*.

The Suburban Gardener and Villa Companion focuses not only on large estate gardens and urban villas, but the smaller gardens of the rising English middle class. Loudon was one of the first to understand the social implications of gardens and the growing importance of botany as a science. He divided houses into "seats," and rated them according to size of the property. His different categories referred to those of the landed gentry, the aristocracy, and the residences of the middle classes. A first rate property had a park and "farmery" and at least 50 acres. A second rate villa was detached on every side but was still part of a row. A third rate was semi-detached and a fourth rate is what is now called "a terrace house," and had less than an acre. Incidentally Loudon described his own home at Portchester Terrace in Bayswater as fourth rate.

A first edition of the 1838 *Suburban Gardener and Villa Companion*, is valued today at $600 plus.

Jane Loudon wrote books for women gardeners. Her first, *Botany for Ladies*, was published in 1842.

The Loudons' writings greatly influenced the tastes of the new middle class and soon England was carpeted with flowers. The Loudons coined the phrase "riot of colour," referring to masses of flowers and by the 1860s, gardeners were using another Loudon phrase "carpet bedding" to refer to gardens filled with flowers.

In addition many famous English writers wrote expansively about their own gardens. Among the most famous was Alexander Pope (1688-1744) who created a famous and influential garden with a lavish grotto at his home at Twickenham, Middlesex.

Another poet, William Shenstone (1714-1763) created an extraordinary garden in the "picturesque" or "ferme ornee" style at his home, The Leasomes, near Birmingham, and perhaps the best known and most prolific garden/literary writer was Vita Sackville-West. She was not only an important member of the Bloomsbury Group, and a friend of Virginia Woolf, but she was an ardent gardener and wrote extensively about her gardens at Sissinghurst. She and her sister, Vanessa Bell, also created a wonderful garden at Charleston, their country home outside of Lewes in southern England.

By the end of the nineteenth century, gardens were a symbol of wealth, and it was very fashionable for gentlemen to study the aesthetics of gardening. Soon a new class of gardener emerged, the gentlemen gardener and the amateur botanist.

Garden books have long been a popular collectible, and collectors have cherished these vintage books not only for their information but for their beautifully embossed covers, elaborate drawings, and botanical illustrations. When detached and framed many of these illustrations have an intrinsic value of their own and are worth between $75 and $150. Gardening magazines vary in price depending on age, condition, and the number and quality of their illustrations. Ordinary twentieth century magazines range in price from $15-$25.

Copies of John and Jane Loudon's books and magazines range in price from $100- $150. Jane Loudon's gardening book for women gardeners is valued at $150-$200 depending on condition.

One of the earliest and most desirable books was *Le Bon Jardiniere*, which was published in the late 1790s in France. While the earliest editions had no illustrations, they had detailed instructions describing how to make specific tools. In 1810 the book included illustrations with their descriptions. This book is valued today at $450 plus.

Books such as James Mangles' *The Floral Calendar, Monthly and Daily, Details Relative To Plants And Flowers, Gardens and Greenhouses, Horticulture And Botany, Aviaries, Etc.,* which was printed in 1839 for private distribution, now sells for $2,500. This volume provides detailed information on the use of flowers for decorative effect inside the home, as well as providing valuable lists of contemporary nurserymen and their specialties. It includes color plates, which show such details as the use of potted plants in window and exterior displays.

There were also many illustrated botany books for children. A particularly desirable one was a French botany and gardening book, *Anonymous Botanique de la Jeunesse,* which was published in Paris in 1812 and is now valued at $750.00 plus.

My Summer in a Garden was published in 1870, $75-100. *Courtesy of The Sugarplum.*

Courtesy of The Sugarplum.

The Home Garden is a vintage 1917 English gardening book, $50-60. *Courtesy of The Sugarplum.*

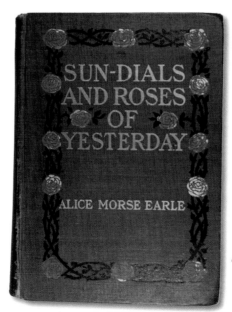

Courtesy of The Sugarplum.

S.O. Beeton and Gertrude Jekyll (1843-1932) were popular authorities on gardening in the late nineteenth century. The Beeton book of *Garden Management* was first published in the early 1860s as *Every Day Gardening*. It was later revised and expanded and became a classic book for more than thirty years. The last revision was in the 1890s.

Gertrude Jekyll was considered one of the doyennes of English gardening. Her gardens were legendary and her books, *Home and Garden*, (1900), *Wood and Garden*, (1910) and *Garden Ornament* (1918) were, for much of the first half of the twentieth century, considered gardening bibles for the up-to-date gardener. Jekyll wrote over fifteen books and today these books are prized by collectors and are among the most sought after vintage gardening books. Some of the other titles were *Children and Gardens*, *Gardens for Small Country Houses*, and *Colour Schemes for the Flower Garden*. First edition Jekyll books are valued between $250-$350. *Garden Ornaments* is one of her rarest and is valued by book collectors at $450 -$500.

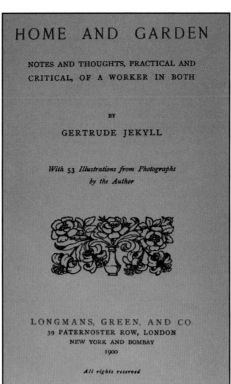

Home and Garden, which was written in 1900 by Gertrude Jekyll, is a very collectible gardening book and sells today for $150-200. *Courtesy of The Sugarplum.*

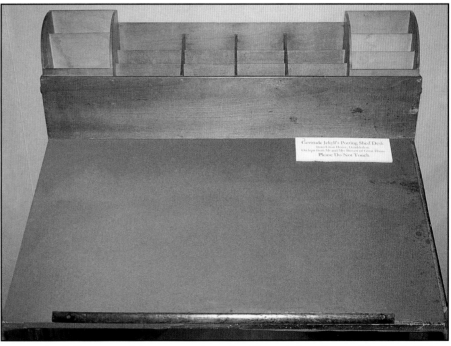

Gertrude Jekyll was one of the most popular and visible English gardeners of the first half of the 20th century. Her writings on gardens were very influential in both England and America. This desk which she used in her potting shed was bought from the sale of her home at Munstead Wood and given to the Museum of Garden History in 1947. It is plain with a sloping top covered with felt and has vertical pigeon holes for paper and pencils.

About two dozen of Gertrude Jekyll's gardens still exist and are open to the public. Most of these have undergone restoration and replanting, and since some of her plants are no longer available, the new plantings are actually "in the style of" Jekyll rather than by Gertrude Jekyll. One of the best restorations was Rosamund Wallinger's 1981 work at The Manor House, Upton Grey, Basingstoke, Hampshire, England.

Glebe House in Woodbury, Connecticut has a "Jekyll designed" garden. In 1926 Jekyll was asked to create an old fashioned garden design. But since many of her plants were not suitable to the New England climate, the plan was modified.

19

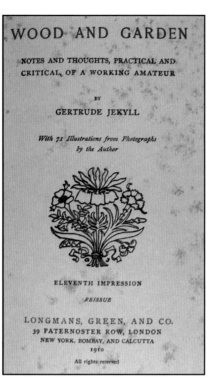

Wood and Garden, which was written in 1910 by Gertrude Jekyll, is now valued at $150-300. Courtesy of The Sugarplum.

The Amateur Kitchen Gardener was written by Shirley Hibberd. Hibberd was a prolific late Victorian garden writer who greatly influenced contemporary garden taste. His Rustic Adornments for Homes of Taste was probably the most influential book published in terms of establishing late nineteenth century English and American tastes for "decorative garden accessories" and parlor gardening. $75-100.

(James) Shirley Hibberd was a prolific late Victorian garden writer who greatly influenced nineteenth century English and American tastes. His book, *Rustic Adornments for Homes of Taste*, which was published in 1895, was probably the most influential book of the day on decorative garden accessories and parlor gardening. The book now sells for $300 plus.

His most famous and most successful book was *The Ivy: A Monograph; Comprising the History, Uses, Characteristics, and Affinities of the Plant, and a Descriptive List of All the Garden Ivies in Cultivation*. Illustrated with colored Plates and Wood Engravings, it was printed in London in 1872. A first edition now sells for $375. *Familiar Gardens*, which was published in 1880 was also a favorite and now sells for $450 plus.

Generally nineteenth and early twentieth century gardening books are noteworthy for their elaborate leather bindings and cover designs. Many had stylized flowers and intertwined vines and plantings. Vintage gardening books range in value from $50-$100. When buying books note that many of these old books have been reprinted by garden clubs or other groups. Check all publication dates.

20th century. Courtesy of The Sugarplum.

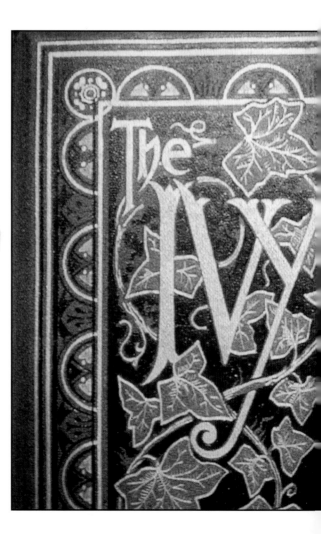

Courtesy of The Sugarplum.

Courtesy of The Sugarplum.

Opposite page, bottom right:
This is the highly decorative and
embossed cover of Shirley Hibberd's
book, *The Ivy. A Monograph;
Comprising the History, Uses,
Characteristics, and Affinities of the
Plant, and a Descriptive List of All
the Garden Ivies in Cultivation.* It is
illustrated with colored plates and
wood engravings. It was published in
London by Groombridge & Sons in
1872. A first edition sells for $375
plus. *The Ivy* was one of Hibberd's
most successful works. Its elaborate
and highly decorative cover was
described as "a contribution to the
book arts as well as horticultural
literature." *Courtesy of Hinck and
Wall.*

My Garden, a 1940s English gardening magazine, $25-40.

A 20th century gardening magazine for children.
Gardening was often a family activity among the
middle class and children were encouraged to help
their parents, particularly their fathers in learning to
identify flowers and plants. Upper class families also
enjoyed gardening and considered a garden as a
necessary status symbol of wealth, but since they
often employed a large gardening staff there wasn't as
much of a hands-on experience.

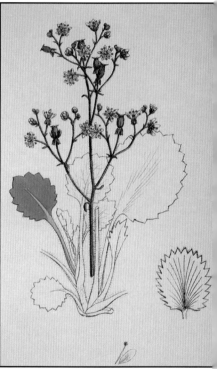

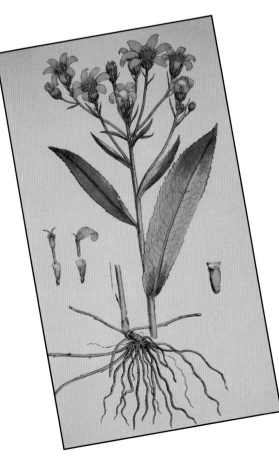

THE
GARDENER'S ASSISTANT:

PRACTICAL AND SCIENTIFIC.

A GUIDE TO THE FORMATION AND MANAGEMENT OF
THE KITCHEN, FRUIT, AND FLOWER GARDENS, AND THE CULTIVATION OF CONSERVATORY,
GREENHOUSE, AND STOVE PLANTS;
WITH A COPIOUS CALENDAR OF GARDENING OPERATIONS, AND SELECT LISTS OF
PLANTS, FRUITS, AND VEGETABLES.

BY

ROBERT THOMPSON,

OF THE ROYAL HORTICULTURAL SOCIETY'S GARDENS, CHISWICK; CORRESPONDING MEMBER OF THE MASSACHUSETTS
HORTICULTURAL SOCIETY, AND OF THE ROYAL COMMISSION OF POMOLOGY OF BELGIUM.

NEW EDITION, REVISED AND EXTENDED,

BY

THOMAS MOORE, F.L.S.,

CURATOR OF THE CHELSEA BOTANIC GARDEN, CO-EDITOR OF THE "GARDENERS' CHRONICLE,"
AND EDITOR OF THE "FLORIST AND POMOLOGIST."

ASSISTED BY EMINENT PRACTICAL GARDENERS.

ILLUSTRATED BY NUMEROUS ENGRAVINGS AND COLOURED PLATES.

LONDON:
BLACKIE & SON, OLD BAILEY, E.C.;
GLASGOW AND EDINBURGH.
1881.

Magazines

Vintage gardening magazines are still relatively cheap, usually priced at between $2-$10. One of the most popular 1920s English magazines, *Garden Illustrated,* has been priced at $2 a magazine while the more vintage 1830s-1840s *The Floricultural Cabinet & Florist's Magazine* is valued at $8-$12.

American gardening magazines are similarly priced. It is interesting to note that paper ephemera is a fascinating collectible and offers diligent shoppers the opportunity to purchase great value and find fascinating insight into gardening history and the use of specific garden tools.

Botanical Plates

There was such an interest in botany among the French, English, German and Italian upper classes, that soon china and porcelain manufacturers were making dishes with highly detailed botanical designs. This interest was also seen in period fashions, textile designs and manifested in home furnishings by the strong love of flowered chintz fabrics found in English manor houses.

We have not priced these plates because many are one of a kind, and difficult to find.

Botanical plate, 19th century, English, $65-80, Courtesy of Riverbank Antiques.

Botanical Plate, 19th century, English, $80-100. Courtesy of Riverbank Antiques.

White Long flowered Daffodil.

Detail

24

Botanical china tureen, 19th century, English. *Courtesy of Riverbank Antiques.*

Detail.

Flower frog, 19th century, English. *Courtesy of Riverbank Antiques.*

Botanical plate, 19th century, English. $50-70. Courtesy of Riverbank Antiques

Book illustration, 19th century, English. *Courtesy of Riverbank Antiques.*

Porcelain flower, 19th century, English. *Courtesy of Riverbank Antiques.*

Decorative inkwell.

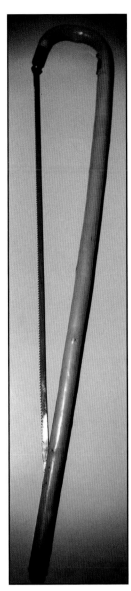

Walking stick tool with saw, c.1910, English. The saw disappears into the wooden handle. Walking stick/saws were first made as early as 1850. *Courtesy of the Museum of Garden History.*

Walking Stick Tools

Walking stick tools became a popular novelty of the middle nineteenth century. These tools had multiple functions. They carried concealed saws, weed whackers, hoes and fruit pickers, and before long it became common to see gentlemen walking with these tools as they inspected their walkways, gardens, and flower borders, disposing of unsightly weeds, stubborn daisies, and even picking ripe pieces of fruit.

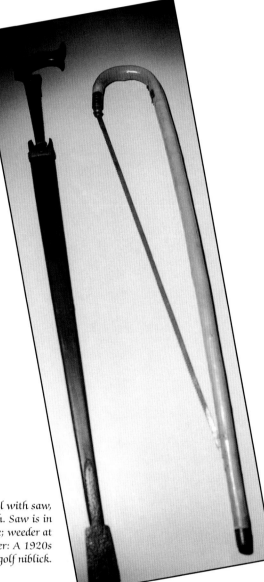

Walking stick tool with saw, c. 1850, English. Saw is in the wooden case; weeder at the end of the other. A 1920s version included a golf niblick.

Walking stick tools, c. 1900, English, made by Thomas Ibbotson, Sheffield, England. One tool has an antler handle, the other has an iron slasher at the end. Small branches etc. could be cut with the slasher-end while taking a stroll.

27

Vintage Postcards

Vintage Victorian and Edwardian gardening postcards are very collectible. The Edwardian landed gentry often had photographs taken of their estates printed with a postcard format on the back. The owners and their guests often used these as notes and sent them in the mail. Since it was so cheap, one half penny, to mail as a postcard in Edwardian times, the staff used these cards to communicate with their families.

Collectors seek cards which offer social commentary or offer an insight into the garden history of the period. Ordinary English gardening postcards from the 1905-1930s are usually priced from $2- $5. Postcards that show aspects of gardening life or offer commentary on social history command higher prices. Shop fronts such as florist shops or ironmongers showing their stocks of watering cans or wheelbarrows can cost between $35 and $50 apiece depending on detail. Images with men and women in a trade are about $15-$30. Cards that show aspects of beekeeping and images of children using tools push up the prices to $6-$15. In the following chapter one of the rarest is that of a horse in his horse boots pulling a

lawn mower. This card is valued at $25 because it is very rare to find a picture of a horse wearing clearly identifiable "boots." Ordinary views of gardens or gardens in public parks are very common and these bring in lower prices and can be purchased for under $1. Postcards and paper ephemera are highly collectible because they are cheap, easy to store and easy to display.

Since Edwardian postcards are usually found at paper and ephemera shows, most garden tool dealers do not carry them. Finding them requires too much time and energy shifting through piles of generic postcards to find garden ones.

Vintage postcard, Edwardian, English, Estate photograph, $5-10, Courtesy of the Museum of Garden History.

Vintage postcard, Edwardian, English, Estate photograph, $5-10, The landed gentry often had photographs taken of their estates. It was common for these photographs to be printed in postcard format and used by the owners, their houseguests and their gardening staff as notecards. Since the postage was so cheap, a halfpenny, the staff sent them out in a smaller size as greeting cards. Courtesy of the Museum of Garden History.

2

Beginning a Garden: Sowing Seeds

Photo by Monika Dorman.

Seed companies have been in business in England since the mid-nineteenth century. One of the earliest English companies was Carters Seeds which was founded in 1836 on High Holborn Street in London. The best known American seed nursery of the early nineteenth century was William Prince and Sons of Flushing, New York. One of their 1834 seed catalogs lists fourteen pages of vegetable seeds, but only five pages for flower seeds. It is important to note that until the mid-nineteenth century, most home gardens grew more herbs and vegetables than flowers. Among the best known nineteenth and early twentieth century American seed manufacturers were the Tillinghast Seed Company in LaConner, Washington, the W. Atlee Burpee Company outside of Philadelphia, and the D.M. Ferry & Company of Detroit.

Advertising poster, c. 1900, American. The Victorians used young children to advertise many products, even tobacco and beer.

Tillinghast Seed Company which was established in 1865, is an American seed distributing company in LaConner, Washington, one of the biggest bulb producing areas in the United States.

Yates Seeds display box. *Courtesy of the Museum of Garden History.*

Winnowing dishes, English, early 20th century. These tin dishes came from Carters Seeds of Raynes Park, London. *Courtesy of the Museum of Garden History.*

Cannell, Carters, Toogood, Sutton, Follows and Bates, Hugh Dickson, W. Saynor Ltd., Benjamin Reid and Company, Woolworth, Yates and Unwin Seeds were English companies. Vilmorin-Andrieux & Company and Les Grains des Paysans were their French contemporaries.

Garden Tools & Seed Catalogs

The growth of flower gardens in Britain got another boost when the "penny post" arrived in Britain in 1840. A cheaper mail service was the impetus for the development of a mail-order seed business. By the late nineteenth century there were several mail-order seed businesses in existence.

Some of the catalogs quoted in this book were from the following companies:

Louis G. Ford was a hardware/general store with six outlets in southern England in 1953.

Sutton & Sons was founded by John Sutton (1777-1863) in Reading, England in 1806. The company is still in existence, based in Hampshire, England.

Carters Seeds is an old, and very historic English seed company. It was founded in 1836 by James Carter (1797-1855). Its first shop was located at 238 High Holborn Street in London. In the 1840s, Carter opened a nursery at Raynes Park, in South London for the propagation of seeds. This was one of the earliest mail order seed companies. The firm remained in existence as Carters through the 1970s when it was taken over by Cooper's. Today it is located in Devon, England.

Unwin Seeds was founded in 1903 by Charles Unwin at Histon, Cambridgeshire.

In 1909, William Wood & Sons were named "The Royal Horticulturists (to George V) and as "Manufacturers , Inventors, Landscape Gardeners &Experts' Purveyors of all Horticultural Requisites." The company was based in Wood Green, north London.

Ordinary late nineteenth and early twentieth century garden seed catalogs offer potential value and are an untapped market for collectors and of particular interest to students of garden history. In researching this book we found old catalogs to be wonderful sources of information.

Vintage seed catalogs are valued for their illustrations, rarity, age, and condition. Generally they are worth $30-$150 a piece. If they have an addendum of tool advertisements at the end of the catalog, they are worth more. If they have full pages of color lithographs they can be worth upwards of $400. An 1834 seed catalog from the American nursery, William Prince and Sons, sells for $1500 plus. Seed packets are worth about $10-$35. American seed packets c. 1910-1920 sell for $7-$15. Vintage English seed packets sell for $3-$10.

Illustrated tool catalogs are extremely valuable and rare. They are valued at $150-$300.

Courtesy of the Museum of Garden History.

Carters Seeds were based in
Raynes Park, London. A
1898 English, Carters seed
catalog. $35-50. *Courtesy of
the Museum of Garden
History.*

*Courtesy of the Museum of
Garden History.*

Early 20th century, American seed
catalogs. Tillinghast seed catalog
collection, La Conner, Washington.
$35-50 each.

1950s English seed catalog, W. French Co. Exeter, England. *Courtesy of the Museum of Garden History.*

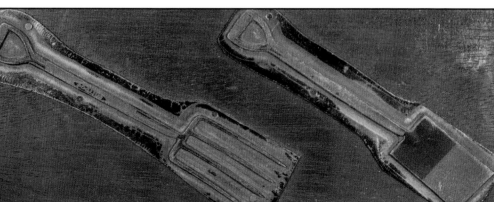

A 1954 Canells vegetable and flower seed catalog. *Courtesy of the Museum of Garden History.*

Ortho Garden Digest, 1954. *Courtesy of the Museum of Garden History.*

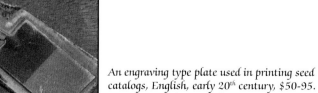

An engraving type plate used in printing seed catalogs, English, early 20th century, $50-95. *Courtesy of The Sugarplum.*

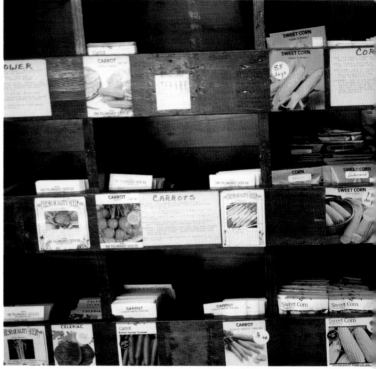

Tillinghast Seeds, 1999, American.

Seed separator, 19th century, American. *Courtesy of Tillinghast Seed Company Collection.*

Tillinghast Seeds, 1999, American.

Carters seed packets, 1952-1971. *Courtesy of the Museum of Garden History.*

Courtesy of the Museum of Garden History.

Carters seed packets, 1952-1971, *Courtesy of the Museum of Garden History.*

Seed packets, 19th century, French, $15-20. *Courtesy of The Sugarplum.*

English, 20th century.

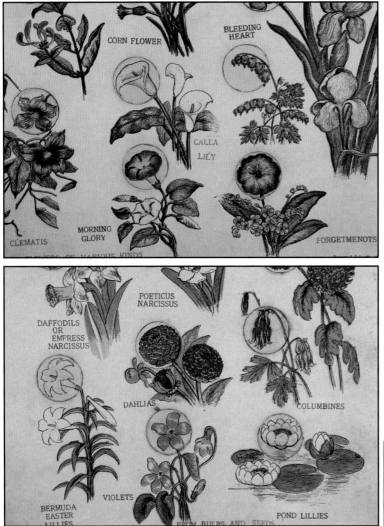

Inside cards. Flower disks are punched out to play the game. *Courtesy of The Sugarplum.*

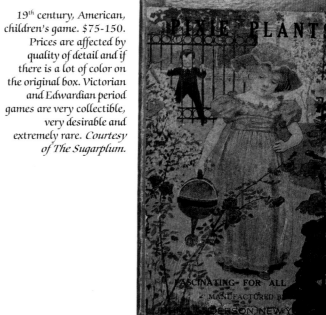

Floral birthday cards, 20th century.

Seed Sowers, Seed Drills, & Seed Planters.

Seed drills, seed sowers and seed planters all have the same function, the mechanical planting of seeds. But usually the term "seed drill" connotes a more agricultural use such as planting seeds over a larger area. A seed sower is usually used in a smaller garden. The mechanical wheeled seed drill dates from 1700.

Seed dispenser, Market Drayton, England, 19th–20th century, English. It has a revolving iron dispenser that contains a seed reservoir. *Courtesy of the Museum of Garden History.*

Seed drills are usually collected for curiosity and not for present day use and unless they have historical significance, are priced between $50-$85.

Dating these tools can be difficult. Turned wooden handles usually were late nineteenth century.

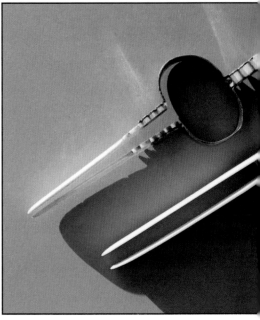

Left: Seed sowers. Left: "So Easy" seed sower manufactured by British Plasticon Products, Birmingham, England, c. 1935. Middle: seed sower manufactured by Rapitest LTD, Clywyd Wales, 1995, Welsh. Right: seed sower printed label, "Robinson's Seed sower manufactured in Maidstone , England. Point arrow to size of hole required for seed distribution." C. 1950.

Below: Corn and potato seed drills, American, early 20 century, $75-100. These drills were designed for plant sowing in fields and larger garden spaces. Note the primitive but intricate mechanisms of these instrument. The D shaped handles were designed for better grips. T shaped handles were better for pushing and digging. *Courtesy of Riverbank Antiques.*

Seed sower, 19th century, English. *Courtesy of the Museum of Garden History.*

Ivory seed tweezers, dibbers and dispensers, c. 1900, (late 19th century-early 20th century), English. These delicate instruments were used to separate the seeds and place them in containers and also prick the soil and plant seeds in the ground. *Courtesy of the Museum of Garden History.*

Little Planet Jr. Seeder, U.S. A. c. 1910, $250-300. *Courtesy of Riverbank Antiques.*

Corn planter, American, 19th century. *Collection of Range Riders Museum, Miles City, Montana.*

Detail.

Harrow for planting seeds.

Detail.

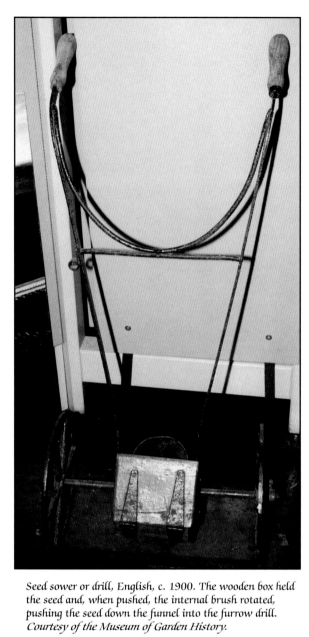

Detail.

Seed cultivator, 19th-20th century, English. *Courtesy of The Sugarplum.*

Seed sower or drill, English, c. 1900. The wooden box held the seed and, when pushed, the internal brush rotated, pushing the seed down the funnel into the furrow drill. *Courtesy of the Museum of Garden History.*

Hand cultivator, early 20th century, American, $40-60. *Courtesy of The Sugarplum.*

Seed cultivator, 19th century, American. *Courtesy of Riverbank Antiques.*

photo by Monika Dorman.

Planting a Garden:
Digging and Cultivating Tools

19th century English.
Courtesy of the Museum of Garden History.

Hand cultivators, 1940s, English. Note the variety in the prongs/fingers. These are English, machine age, mass-produced garden tools commonly used in the 1940s-1950s. They are also painted in popular gardening colors-reds and greens. The fingers mimic the motions and positions of a hand in stirring and cultivating the soil to get it ready for planting. These tools range in price from $15-45 depending on condition, novelty and design. Since gardening is so hands-on, it is important to have tools that can function in different garden spaces.

Hand Forks, Claws, Weeders, & Hand Cultivators

Hand tools with finger-like appendages have become one of the most essential tools of gardeners. Americans tend to call these instruments "hand forks," "hand rakes," or "hand cultivators." English gardeners call these short handled tools, "weeders" or "claws." Often the words "hand shovel," "hand spade," or "trowel" are interchangeable.

We have found a variety of prices for these tools depending on condition, paint, amount of rusting and variety of its designs. The position of the prongs or fingers also effect value. American makers tend to make a four-pronged rake. The English like three pronged and twisted prongs. A Canterbury hoe was a hoe with three "stout" prongs and was used to break up cultivated soil prior to new plantings.

Prices of old tools vary according to where they have been found. In flea markets, they can be picked out of a bin, and purchased for $10-$25. Garden shops that specialize in gardening tools and antiques will charge up to $65. Early forks have iron heads and wooden handles. Tools were "japanned" or painted as early as the mid-nineteenth century. Mid-twentieth century tools were made of steel, stainless steel or aluminum. The handles of American-made tools from the 1940s-1950s were often painted in bright reds, greens, blues or yellows.

There is no limit to the inventiveness and ingenuity of garden tools. Tools came in different sizes and forms. Some were truly extensions of the gardener's arms designed to enlarge his reach as well as enable him to maneuver into tight spaces. One of the most ingenious tools was the twentieth century dual-purpose rake/shovel. This flexible tool was designed for efficiency. Just flip it over and you can do anything.

When examining garden tools, it is important to note that their "prongs" mimic the motions and positions of a hand digging, weeding, cultivating and planting the soil.

Hand cultivator/hand fork, 1940s-1950s, American, $25-35. Note the green wooden handle. Green was a popular color in the 1940s.

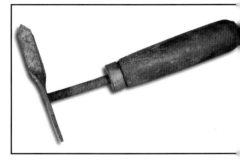

Hand cultivator, 19th century-early 20th century, English, $15-25. *Courtesy of Riverbank Antiques.*

Hand weeders, 19th century, English. Top: onion hoe. Notice that the exaggerated position of these tools allow for more flexibility and give the gardener the ability to reach into difficult corners. Gardeners need to reach into window boxes, far corners of small plots and behind plants already in place. These tools are worth between $45-80.

Hand weeder, 19th-early 20th century, English. *Courtesy of the Museum of Garden History.*

Hand fork or cultivator, 20th century, English. *Courtesy of the Museum of Garden History.*

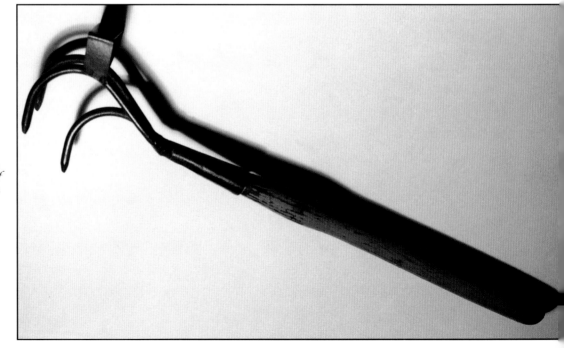

Hand tools, 1940s-1950s, *Courtesy of Gramercy Tavern, Roberta BenDavid Designs.*

43

English weeders, 19th-20th century English. *Courtesy of the Museum of Garden History.*

44

Hand forks/weeders/cultivators, painted red, 20th century, English. The right handfork has "twisted prongs."

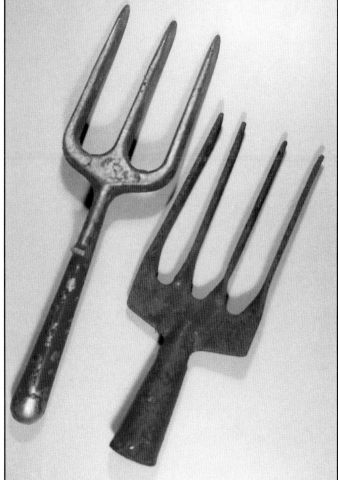

Hand forks, 1890-1940, English. Note the differences in the design of the prongs. Each of these forks has a plant specific function. *Courtesy of Riverbank Antiques.*

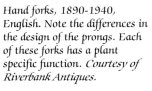

Weeding forks, 20th century, c. 1940-1950, English, painted red , $35-50. Forks were made with three or four prongs. The extra prong helped aerate the soil. Three prongs were sturdier and worked the soil better. Note that the top fork has twisted prongs and is missing its handle. *Courtesy of The Sugarplum.*

Hand fork, 20th century, English. *Courtesy of Riverbank Antiques.*

Garden tools come in many sized handles for different jobs. 20th century English. *Courtesy of The Sugarplum.*

Note the intricate carved design of the handle.
1940s. *Courtesy of The Sugarplum.*

Hand fork/weeding fork with twisted
prongs, 1920-1940, English, $35-50.
Courtesy of The Sugarplum.

Weeding fork, 1920-1930. This fork is
designed to reach into difficult spaces.

Hand fork, 20th century, English,
$35-50. *Courtesy of The Sugarplum.*

Hand rake, English, c. 1900, $35-75. *Courtesy of The Sugarplum.*

Detail.

Hand fork or weeding fork with short handle, mid-19th century, English, $30-50. *Courtesy of The Sugarplum.*

Hand rake, English, c. 1900, $35-75.

Courtesy of Gramercy Tavern, Roberta BenDavid Designs.

20th century, English. *Courtesy of The Sugarplum.*

47

Photo by Monika Dorman.

The early Romans used spades and trowels made out of wood and bone and later iron. Trowels as we know them today were probably first used in the 1700s by stone masons or bricklayers. By 1800, they were being used by gardeners as a form of hand rake. The earliest versions were just long pieces of semi-circular metal with handles. Beginning in the eighteenth century, trowels began to undergo design variations and soon had specific functions. One of the most specific was the fern trowel, designed to dig in rocky crevices.

These hatchets are late 19th-mid-20th century. Many have letter stamps. One is probably a plasterer's hatchet. The others have woodland/garden uses. In design they are similar to mattocks. The *Courtesy of the Museum of Garden History.*

Mattocks/spade double blade, 19th century, English. Many spade blades were double headed so that the gardener could be flexible when working in difficult, rocky soil. *Courtesy of the Museum of Garden History.*

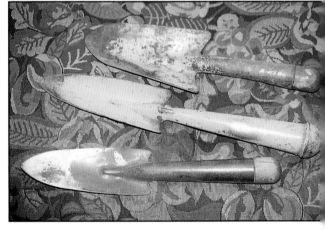

Courtesy of Gramercy Tavern. Roberta BenDavid Designs.

Courtesy of Gramercy Tavern. Roberta BenDavid Designs.

Dibbers are one of the most ancient garden tools and originally were long sticks or poles with a sharpened point made out of a rock or a bone and used to dig a hole to plant seeds or bulbs. They were originally called "setting stykes." The word dibber is probably a Kentish dialect variation of the original word "debbyll," or "dabby." As early as 1570 a garden writer was referring to "dibbers," rakes, mattocks, hoes, levels, and spades.

Gradually dibbers became more and more refined pointed sticks with heavy-duty metal points. The Norwegians carved elaborate designs on their dibbers. Today dibbers are used most often for crops such as potatoes. While most dibbers have heavy-duty metal pointed ends, others are more delicate and made of ivory. These smaller dibbers were used to prick the soil with tiny holes for planting individual seeds.

Before the days of mass production, garden tools were made by hand, often by the individual gardener, the local blacksmith or the ironmonger. Either the blacksmith would improvise or follow the directions found in early eighteenth and nineteenth century gardening books. These books included detailed plans on making tools and, after 1810, detailed illustrations offering gardeners advice as to which tools would be best for specific tasks, how to make the tools, and which materials were the most durable.

It is interesting to note that soon many tools developed a regional stylization since gardeners would share their tools with their neighbors, borrow friends' tools or buy them from the same blacksmith. Often blacksmiths would make copies and sell them to others in the area, and before long each region developed specific design characteristics as tool designs became localized.

As late as 1927, a Sheffield toolmaker, C.T. Skelton made spades, forks and other tools in at least five regional styles: Cheshire, Guernsey, Irish, Kentish, and Scotch. A three-pronged fork with three stout, flattened tines came to be known as a "Canterbury hoe."

Garden tools are classified by size, function, task or handle. Tools either had plain pole handles, "D"-shaped handles or "T"-shaped handles. Inventories of nineteenth or twentieth century garden tools note the variety of chore-specific blades as well as chore specific handles. Since gardening tasks are either push-pull, pull away, or push, the cutting edges of blades were angled accordingly. The cutting edge of a tool's blade influenced function. If the inner edge of a blade was sharp, then the direction was pull. If the blade had a sharpened outer edge, then the direction was push away. Dutch hoes were designed to push through the dirt, while torpedo hoes were designed to push and pull it away.

Hand tools either have wooden or iron handles. The smaller red spade was useful for delicate plantings whereas the larger more rugged spade would be more useful in larger planting areas, $30-35. Courtesy of The Sugarplum.

Hand rake, trowel, two hand spades, and a smaller trowel, 1940s-1950s, American, $35-45. These tools have traces of their original paint. Green and red were the most popular colors. Spades and trowels were manufactured in many different shapes allowing the gardener to get into difficult, hard to reach or small spaces such as window boxes, hanging baskets, or urns. Courtesy of Riverbank Antiques.

These hand spades have elevated handles to allow the gardener to reach down into a difficult spot. Notice the variety of handles. Some are thick. Others have slimmer handles. Often wooden handles rotted away and makeshift replacements had to be made. Due to their poor condition, these shovels are valued at $15-25. *Courtesy of Riverbank Antiques.*

Planting spade, 20th century, English, $45-60. The smaller sized spade has a flattened rim, and an unusual "T" shaped handle, which suggests that it was designed to push dirt as well as dig. Garden tools either have plain pole handles or "D" or "T" shaped handles. *Courtesy of the Museum of Garden History.*

Trowel, American, 19th-20th century, $35-45. This seems to be a makeshift replacement handle. *Courtesy of Riverbank Antiques.*

Hand spade, c.1870, English, $40-95. This very rare "T" shaped handled spade has what looks like a makeshift handle that has been cut down from a larger and longer tool. Again this snout-shaped rim indicates that this tool would be used for pushing dirt away. *Courtesy of The Sugarplum.*

50

Each of these different shapes reflect an adaptation for a different function, English, late 19th-early 20th century, $25-45. *Courtesy of The Sugarplum.*

Vegetables such as scallions and garlic need more delicate shovels than do heartier crops such as potatoes and beets.

Spade, American, 20th century, $25-30. The incline of the spade was designed to reach into more difficult spaces. *Courtesy of Riverbank Antiques.*

Fern trowel, late 19th century-early half of 20th century, English, $50-65. Fern trowels removed ferns from crevices. They were also used to transplant seedlings and cuttings. *Courtesy of The Sugarplum.*

Three 19th century English claws. Left: A single purpose claw/weeder/cultivator. Middle: a dual-purpose claw/spade. Right: A dual-purpose hand rake/spade. *Courtesy of the Museum of Garden History.*

Double-headed

TWO HEADS-
TO HOE EITHE
A ROW OF PL

Swoe

INVENTED B
COMPANY
RATHER LIK

Mattock

THIS IS WHA
CALL A

Another rake/claw.

Left: fern trowel or bulb planter, English, c. 1890, $50-65. Right: hand fork with flattened tines, English, c. 1900, $35-40. These tines were probably useful for breaking up the soil. Flattened tines were often used to dig up carrots or potatoes. *Courtesy of The Sugarplum.*

A page from a 1905 Carters catalog, English. *Courtesy of the Museum of Garden History.*

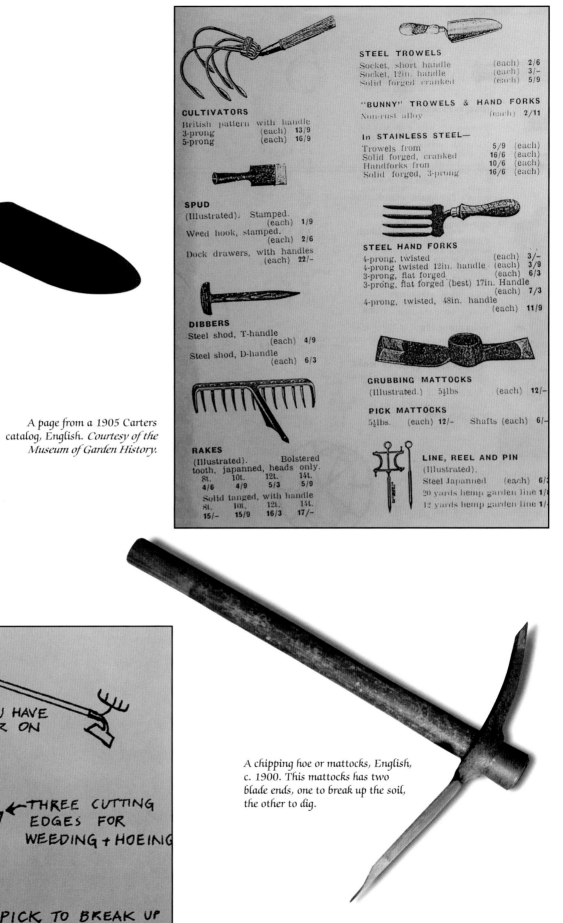

STEEL TROWELS
Socket, short handle   (each) 2/6
Socket, 12in. handle   (each) 3/-
Solid forged cranked   (each) 5/9

"BUNNY" TROWELS & HAND FORKS
Non-rust alloy   (each) 2/11

In STAINLESS STEEL—
Trowels from   5/9 (each)
Solid forged, cranked   16/6 (each)
Handforks from   10/6 (each)
Solid forged, 3-prong   16/6 (each)

CULTIVATORS
British pattern with handle
3-prong   (each) 13/9
5-prong   (each) 16/9

SPUD
(Illustrated). Stamped.
            (each) 1/9
Weed hook, stamped.
            (each) 2/6
Dock drawers, with handles
            (each) 22/-

STEEL HAND FORKS
4-prong, twisted   (each) 3/-
4-prong twisted 12in. handle.   (each) 3/9
3-prong, flat forged   (each) 6/3
3-prong, flat forged (best) 17in. Handle
                                    (each) 7/3
4-prong, twisted, 48in. handle   (each) 11/9

DIBBERS
Steel shod, T-handle
            (each) 4/9
Steel shod, D-handle
            (each) 6/3

GRUBBING MATTOCKS
(Illustrated.)   5¼lbs   (each) 12/-

PICK MATTOCKS
5¼lbs. (each) 12/-   Shafts (each) 6/-

RAKES
(Illustrated).   Bolstered
tooth, japanned, heads only.
  8t.   10t.   12t.   14t.
  4/6   4/9   5/3   5/9
  Solid tanged, with handle
  8t.   10t.   12t.   14t.
  15/-   15/9   16/3   17/-

LINE, REEL AND PIN
(Illustrated).
Steel Japanned   (each) 6/3
20 yards hemp garden line 1/
12 yards hemp garden line 1/

...rsions could answer this one

FLIP IT OVER & YOU HAVE A CULTIVATOR ON THE BACK

...SON SWORD
... CLUB

THREE CUTTING EDGES FOR WEEDING + HOEING

PICK TO BREAK UP SOIL

BLADE FOR DIGGING

A chipping hoe or mattocks, English, c. 1900. This mattocks has two blade ends, one to break up the soil, the other to dig.

Drawing by Philip Norman.

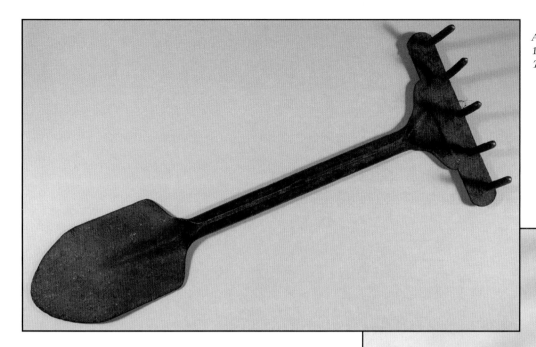

A miniature multi/purpose tool, English, late 19th century-early 20th century. *Courtesy of The Sugarplum.*

Hand spade and handfork, English, late 19th century-early 20th century, $35-50. The handles of these tools are missing. *Courtesy of The Sugarplum.*

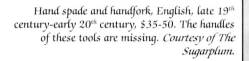

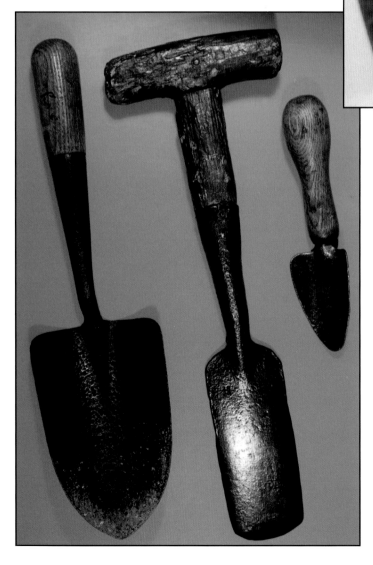

Hand spades. Note that the different sizes were used for different garden spaces. The smallest is more like a dibber than a spade. American and English gardeners use different terms. Often the words "hand shovel," "hand spade," or "trowel" are interchangeable. *Courtesy of the Museum of Garden History.*

Dibber, 19th century, English. *Courtesy of the Museum of Garden History.* Dibbers had pointed ends to dig sharp holes for seeds and bulbs.

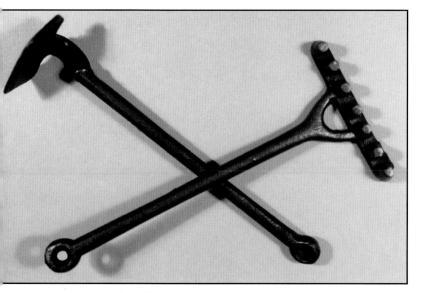

Miniature garden tools, dollhouse sized, English, c. 1880, $40-85. This set is very rare, probably because the tools are so small and could be easily lost or misplaced.

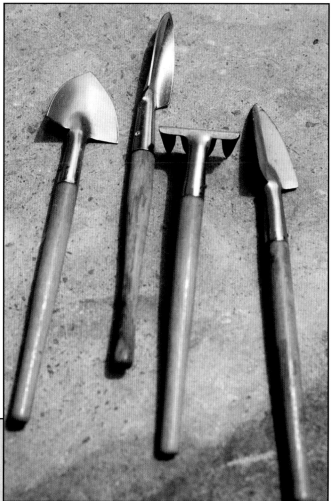

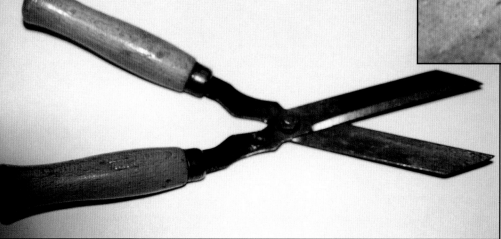

Miniature sized hedge clipper, c.1900, English. *Courtesy of the Museum of Garden History.*

Fern trowels. The one with the bulbous handle as manufactured by James Howarth, Sheffield, England late 19th century. The flatter one c. 1900, English, has a belt loop on the leather sheath so that it is carried at the ready on your belt for plant hunting. *Courtesy of the Museum of Garden History.*

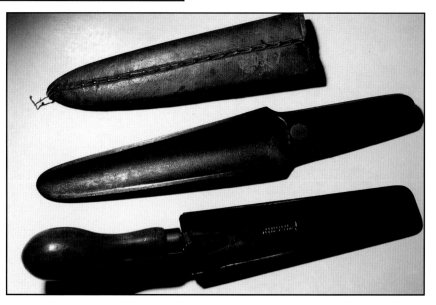

Dibber, 19th–20th century. English. Note the variety of dibber handles. Dibbers are designed to be jabbed into the ground to make a sharp hole. *Courtesy of the Museum of Garden History.*

Bark stripper, English, 1880, $40-85. This tool has been fashioned out of old tool parts. Note the initials of its owner are carved into the handle. *Courtesy of The Sugarplum.*

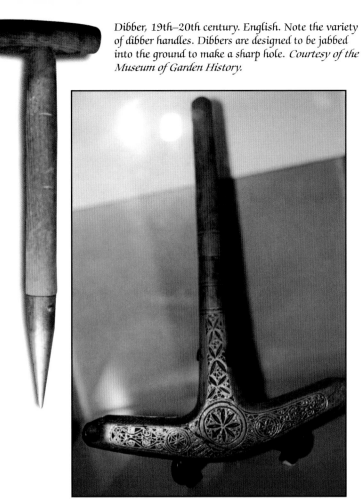

Norwegian dibber, 18th century, carved wood. This is one of the most ornate dibbers we have found.

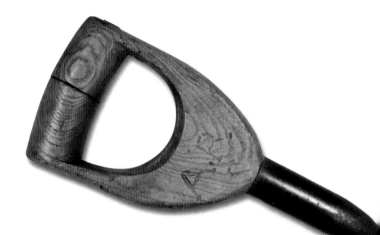

Dibber, 20th century, English, wood, $35-50. This dibber has a simpler "D" shaped and carved initials on the handle. *Courtesy of The Sugarplum.*

Dibber, 20th century, English. *Courtesy of the Museum of Garden History.*

Detail.

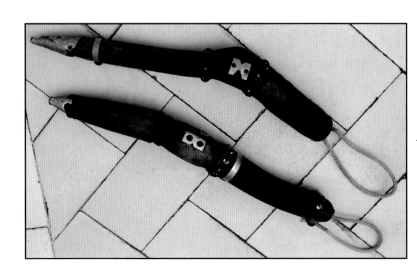

Dibbers, French or English, late 19th-early 20th. These are among the most elaborately designed dibbers we have found for daily use. $65-100. *Courtesy of Riverbank Antiques.*

Dual-purpose dibber/pruner, gardener's knife, late 19th-early 20th century, English, $75-150. *Courtesy of Riverbank Antiques.*

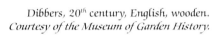

Dibbers, 20th century, English, wooden. *Courtesy of the Museum of Garden History.*

Bulb planter, c. 1950, Sheffield, England. Particularly useful for planting bulbs in grass. A round hole of turf was lifted from the grass by the cutting end and bulbs planted, turf then replaced. *Courtesy of the Museum of Garden History.*

Detail. It is interesting to note that this tool had been painted red.

The fruits of a gardener's labors.

Vintage postcard. Edwardian, English, $10-15. This card shows two of the gardening staff with a child, poised for work with their tools—a mule hoe, a digging hoe, and a rake. The Victorians particularly liked cards and advertisements that showed children with tools. Images of children add value. *Courtesy of the Museum of Garden History.*

Daisy grubber, English, 20th century. Daisy grubbers were very specific tools designed to weed the ubiquitous daisy out of the grass creating a more perfect lawn. Most daisy grubbers had a pivoting action on the bowl to lever the daisies and other weeds out. *Courtesy of the Museum of Garden History.*

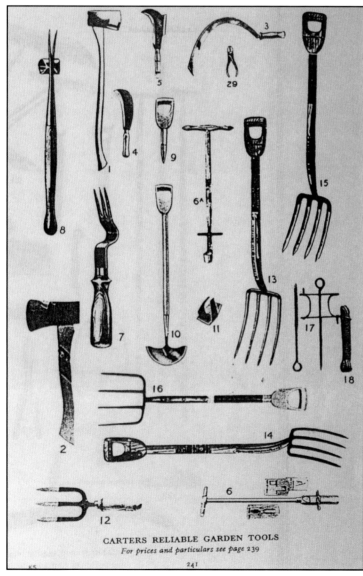

A page from a 1931 Carters Reliable tool catalog, English. *Courtesy of the Museum of Garden History.*

A page from a 1953 Louis Ford tool catalog, English.

Daisy grubber, English, early 20th century. *Courtesy of the Museum of Garden History.*

Long-handled daisy grubber, T-shaped handle, English, late 19th-20th century, $50-75. *Courtesy of The Sugarplum.*

Daisy grubber, English, late 19th century. *Courtesy of the Museum of Garden History.*

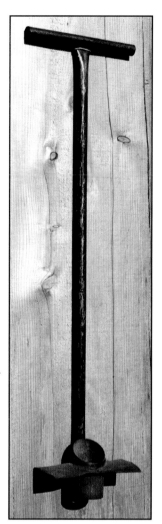

Bulb planting hoe, English, T-shaped handle, 20th century, $65-90. T-shaped handles were more common in tools that required a digging action. *Courtesy of The Sugarplum.*

Daisy grubber, English, late 19th century. *Courtesy of the Museum of Garden History.*

Short-handled Hoes: Potato Hoes, Spud Hoes, Dutch Hoes, Weeding Hoes, Onion Hoes, Moss Scrapers, & Daisy Grubbers

Gardeners have been using hoes since Roman days. The earliest hoe was a simple digging stick attached to a rock or a carved bone. One of the earliest variations of a hoe was a "Canterbury hoe," a three-pronged hoe used to break up or cultivate the soil before planting.

In the 1830s, popular English gardening expert John Loudon suggested that since " a man can draw more than he can push, most heavy work can be easiest done by the drawn hoe."

Other variations were onion, carrot and weeding hoes. A unique variation was the double-headed hoe which enabled the gardener to weed between two rows at the same time. There were two kinds of double–headed hoes, one with a horseshoe type attachment, the other with a blade/cultivator on the end. Beetroot hoes were used to dig around beets. There was also a beet hoe, a long handled hoe with a swan necked upended blade, which was designed to weed in fields between sugar beet.

Two other variations were Dutch hoes which date from before 1850 and "spud hoes." Spud hoes had nothing to do with potatoes, but were designed to pull out weeds. There are two kinds of spud hoe blades; a circular blade and a cleft blade to yank out stubborn weeds from crevices.

By 1850, hoes were being combined with walking sticks. In the 1950s the Wilkinson Sword Company invented a "swoe." This tool, which looked like a golf club, had a blade on either end of the stick each with a different function. The "swoe" could be used in two directions. One end had a blade with three cutting edges for weeding and hoeing.

Tools soon developed into categories according to the length of their handles. Shorter handled tools were more often found in home gardens. They were also were more task specific. Gardeners chose these tools for their specific blade function and for shape and heft of their handles.

Short-handled hoes are particularly fascinating from an artistic point of view. Note the variety of the shapes and angles of these tools. Potato hoes, daisy grubbers, moss scrapers, weeding hoes, and onion hoes all have pronounced angular shapes. Smaller trowels have curved blades that echo the shape of terracotta pots and potting containers. Today tools are more uniform in design. But nineteenth century gardeners knew the differences between short neck, swan-necked, triangle-shaped, and half-moon shaped hoes.

Photo by Monika Dorman.

An onion hoe, 20th century, English. *Courtesy of the Museum of Garden History.*

Spud hoes, 19th century, English. Although these two chisel-like implements were called "spud hoes," they had nothing to do with digging potatoes. They were designed to dig up or cut down weeds like docks, dandelions, etc. and were often made locally from old, large chisel blades. They were first mentioned in the 17th century by famous English diarist Samuel Pepys. These small hoes with their round circular cutting blades were used to dislodge dirt in small spaces such as a window box. *Courtesy of the Museum of Garden History.*

Hand hoes, 19th century, English. The top tool is a weed hook, late 19th century. These cast iron hoe blades were fastened to wooden handles, which are missing. It is common to find the original blades with a newer or makeshift handle. *Courtesy of the Museum of Garden History.*

Half-moon edger, 19th century, English, $60-85. The direction of the cutting edge of this tool's blade influenced its function whether the direction of the motion was push-pull or pull. If the inner edge was sharp then the direction was push-pull. If the tool had a sharpened outer edge then the direction was push. *Courtesy of the Museum of Garden History.*

Torpedo hoe, 19th century, English. This kind of hoe was designed to pull and push the dirt. Torpedo hoes were useful because both sides of the hoe's blade were sharpened and thus you could weed by either pushing the hoe away, or pulling it towards you. Since torpedo hoes had pointed ends, they were very good for the selective culling of individual weeds. *Courtesy of the Museum of Garden History.*

Another view.

Photo by Monika Dorman.

Onion hoe, potato hoe, moss scraper, 19th century. English. *Courtesy of the Museum of Garden History.*

Hand fork, onion hoe, 19th century, English. *Courtesy of the Museum of Garden History.*

Dutch hoes, 19th century-early 20th century, English. These were designed to pull towards you and cultivate the grounds. Note that the handles are missing. There was no uniformity in the length of garden tools since gardeners often cut down the handles of their longer tools to convert them into hand tools, and individualized them to their own height and body proportions. *Courtesy of the Museum of Garden History.*

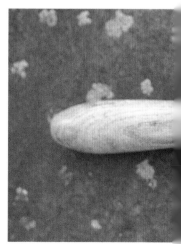

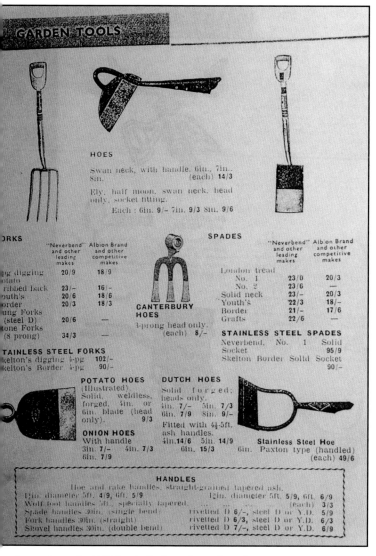

A page from the 1953 Louis Ford garden tool catalog.

Potato Planter, 19th century, American. *Courtesy of the Range Riders Museum, Miles City, Montana*

Photo by Monika Dorman.

Onion hoe, 19th century, English. *Courtesy of the Museum of Garden History.*

63

Long-handled Tools: Rakes, Shovels, Clay and Mule Hoes

Soon there were long handled tools and short handled tools. Longer handled tools were designed to eliminate bending and for the more difficult areas to reach. They helped the gardener reach higher branches in orchards or work in the fields. And when selecting a long handled tool, a gardener was more likely to choose one according to the weight and the length of its handle

Two types of long handled hoes or spades are of particular interest due to the shape of their blades: the mule or clay hoe/spade and the heart shaped turfing iron. There are also long handled dibbers, bulb planters and shovels or spades designed for heavy lifting required for making pathways and borders

Courtesy of Larkspur Farms.

Photo by Monika Dorman.

A variation of a rake head. Note the design of the "teeth." 20th century, American, $35-45. *Courtesy of the Eli Leon Collection.*

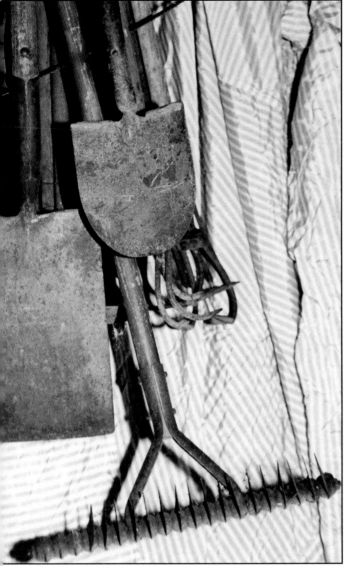

American farm tools, 20th century. *Courtesy of the Eli Leon Collection.*

Hodding spade, 20th century, English, made by W. H. Lyndon, Birmingham, England. A similar shovel was listed in another catalog in the 1960s as a contractors' shovel. Since hod are bricks, perhaps this shovel is not garden related. *Courtesy of the Museum of Garden History.*

Right: Clay or mule spade, c. 1900, English. Clay or mule spades were used for digging heavy soils. Sticky clay is very difficult to dig and the mule ensured that the clay would not adhere to the spade and would come away easily. The blade's openness helped the gardener cultivate more readily. *Courtesy of the Museum of Garden History.*

Left: A D-shaped handle turfing iron, 19th –20th century, English, and a T-shaped handle turfing iron, English. Turfing irons were usually heart-shaped, the shovel part was flatter and lighter than an iron spade. Heart-shaped turfing spades or trenching irons have also been described as Ace of Spade-shaped. The smaller one is Victorian, c.1860, $150-170. This tool has such an ordinary function, but is such a beautiful form. Turfing irons were used to lift turf by pushing under the grass. *Courtesy of the Museum of Garden History.*

Three 19th century long-handled hoes and shovels. Left: clay spade or mule open-faced spade, English, late 19th-20th century, c. 1900. Middle: peat spade, stamped "Harrison, Wisbech," English, c. 1900; Right; trenching spade for drains/ditches, stamped "Skelton," Sheffield, English, c. 1900. The iron "apron" protects the wooden shovel from rotting or chipping in the soil. As late as 1927 C.T. Skelton of Sheffield made thirty-five different kinds of spade, with different finishes and sizes with D and T-shaped handles. It also made thirty-five different forks for asparagus, beetroot, potato, and regional style such as Cheshire, Guernsey, Irish, Kentish, and Scotch. *Courtesy of the Museum of Garden History.*

T-shaped handled shovels, 19th century-20th century, English. The spade on the left is also called a "border spade," $60-85. *Courtesy of the Museum of Garden History.*

Top left: Potato digger, French, early 20th century, $65-75. This tool was designed to dig up potatoes from the field. Notice the gripping mechanism, the lever for the foot to gain stability, and the two-pronged clamp handle. *Courtesy of Riverbank Antiques.*

A field of potato blossoms, LaConner, Washington.

    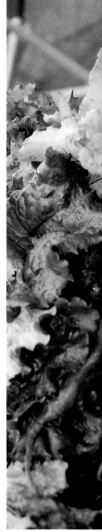

Above, Left to right:
Left: half-moon lawn edger, 19th century, English, $45-60. Right: hoe, 20th century, English, $45-65 depending on condition. *Courtesy of The Sugarplum.*

English, 20th century, $45-65. *Courtesy of The Sugarplum.*

A rake/hoe, c. 1900, English, $45-65. This is called a Prussian patterned hoe and was used to turn the soil. *Courtesy of The Sugarplum.*

Hoe, 20th century, English. This small bladed hoe is designed for delicate plants which need tender care and raking. *Courtesy of The Sugarplum.*

A hoe and an onion hoe, English, 20th century. *Courtesy of Riverbank Antiques.*

Hoes, scythes, and trimmers. *Courtesy of the Museum of Garden History.*

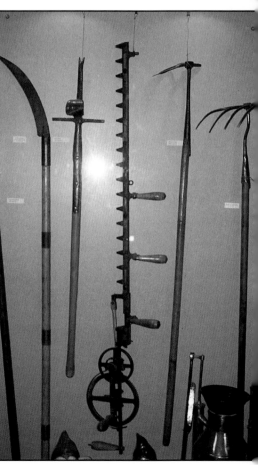

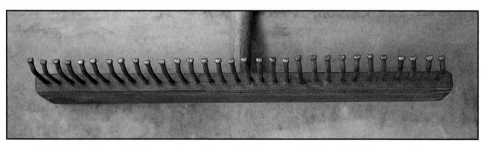

A rake head made out of nails. An intrepid English farmer made this rake during World War II. *Courtesy of the Museum of Garden History.*

There are also many different varieties of scythe blades.

Two smaller bladed hoes, English, 20th century. *Courtesy of The Sugarplum.*

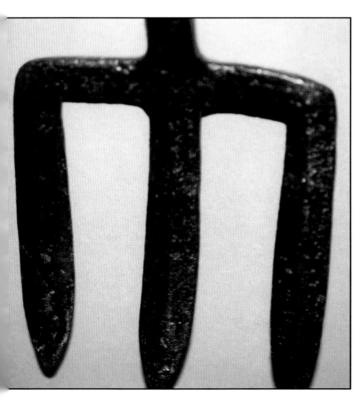

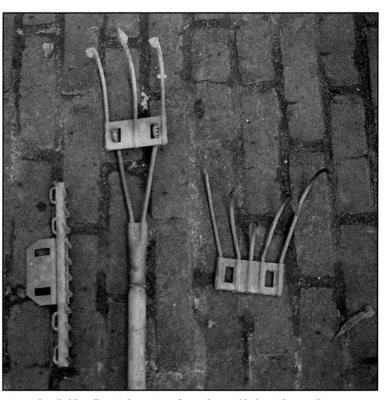

Long-handled handles with a series of attachment blades. Often tools were ordered with a set of attachments that fastened to the pole. *Courtesy of the Museum of Garden History.*

English, late 19th century. Flattened fork tines were used for breaking up the soil that had been previously dug over with a spade or soil in the bottom of a trench. In later years flat tines were used to dig up carrots, potatoes, etc. therefore preventing damage. The handle of this fork was probably replaced later. *Courtesy of the Museum of Garden History.*

Spade, treaded garden spade, (the rolled top edge of the blade is the tread), 19th-20th century, English. $45-65, *Courtesy of Riverbank Antiques.*

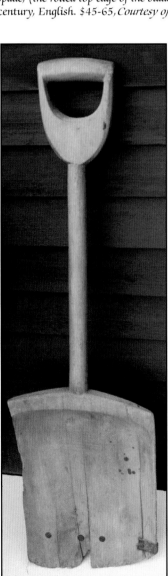

Left, left to right:
A working spade, 20th century, American. *Courtesy of Larkspur Farm, LaConner, Washington.*

A working wooden shovel, English, 19th century, $50-65. *Courtesy of The Sugarplum.*

19th century, English. Note the lift for the shoe to insure stability. *Courtesy of the Museum of Garden History.*

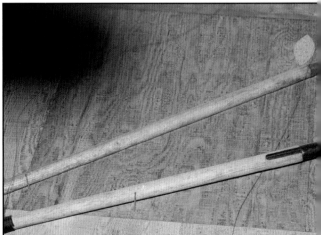

Two and three-tined pitchforks, 19th century, American, $65-75. *Courtesy of Riverbank Antiques.*

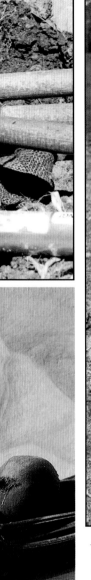

A nineteenth century French illustration. *Courtesy of Hinck and Wall.*

American pitchfork. *Courtesy of The Sugarplum.*

A beet hoe. *Courtesy of the Museum of Garden History.*

Garden forks, late 19th century, English. *Courtesy of the Sugarplum.*

Hoe for sugar beet. *Drawing by Philip Norman.*

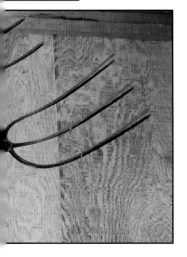

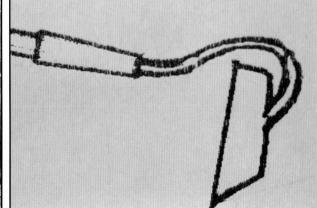

71

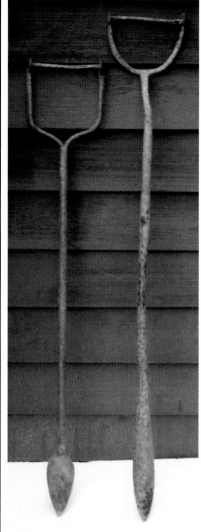

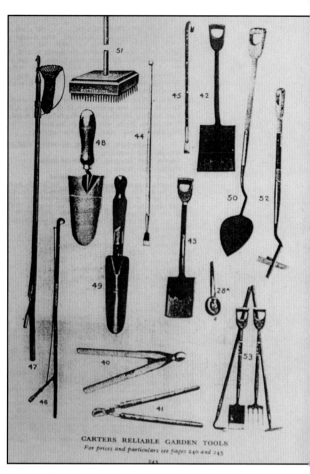

A page from a 1931 *Carters Blue Book of Reliable Tools.* *Courtesy of the Museum of Garden History.*

Garden fork, late 19ᵗʰ century, English. *Courtesy of the Sugarplum.*

D-shaped, Victorian, English turfing spade, $140-160. *Courtesy of The Sugarplum.*

Long-handled dibbers, English, c. 1830, $60-90. *Courtesy of The Sugarplum.*

A page from a 1909 William Wood &Son garden tool catalog.

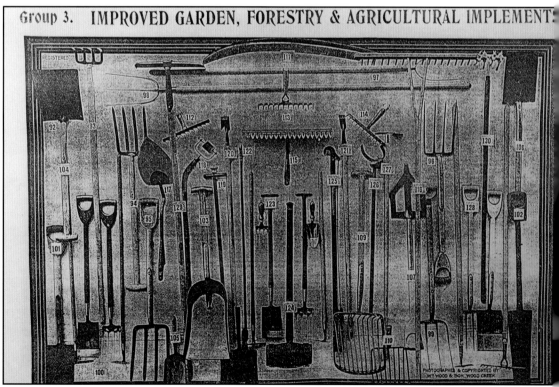

Order in the Garden

Photo by Monika Dorman.

Row Markers, Garden Reels, Edgers, Markers, Plant Labels, & Tallies

Gardeners have always demanded order in their gardens and one of the most efficient ways to define space, maintain boundaries and order in a garden is through the use of garden row markers, also known as garden reels or garden liners. Gardeners would mark their rows by staking twine from a garden reel or row marker in straight rows to plant their crops in neat lines. This enabled a more efficient harvesting, a better use of space, and also created a more appealing visual picture.

Photo by Monika Dorman.

Photo by Monika Dorman.

Plant label storage containers, 19th century, English. These small glass containers were used to protect and store plant labels in the hot house and were manufactured by Bateson Bros, Liverpool. *Courtesy of the Museum of Garden History.*

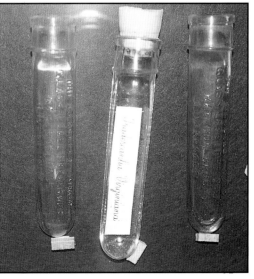

Classic gardens have always been noted for their order and precision. This was dictated by both aesthetic and efficiency reasons. Gardeners marked their gardens as a means of defining property lines as well as making crops more accessible for maintenance and harvesting. Edging tools or garden row markers were essential to define and maintain neat garden paths, walkways, flowerbeds, and flower borders. The earliest garden reels were simple wooden boxes that held the twine that was used to line out the rows, edges and crop divisions.

The Egyptians and ancient Babylonians used tallies to mark their herbs. We know that monks in Pisa and Padua in the sixteenth century grew flowers in a series of small compact beds, and while they did not mark them in the ground, they kept meticulous notes.

Trowel, English c. 1910. This was designed to remove plants from a pot, hence the blade is curved to fit pots and the handle angle is positioned so it will not damage the plant.

We also know that, by the eighteenth century, the French were marking their flowers with tailles or tallies. These early tallies (which kept track of plants) were large wooden sticks with Roman numerals cut into them. The numbers read upwards on the stick.

Plant markers or tallies were made of stone, iron, bone, metal, lead, wood, and earthenware. As early as 1841, an English journal, *The Ladies Home Companion to the Flower Garden* advised their readers that porcelain tallies or labels were better for pots, while lead and cast iron labels or markers were best for plants in the open ground. Later, tallies were made of plastic and glass.

The earliest garden edging forms date from the eighteenth century and were made of terracotta. Popular patterns were rope twists, spirals, gothic arches, fluted edges, and plain rounded forms. They were often made of glazed blue, brown and white Staffordshire. In the nineteenth century, these forms were made of molded metals, cast iron, and galvanized wire. Popular edging forms were either single pieces, connecting arches, or basket rounds. Mass produced border arches of galvanized wire became particularly popular after the Industrial Revolution. By the twentieth century wood and plastic became popular materials. Popular patterns were either spiral, latticed or just simple mesh designs. Border arches came in 9, 12, and 15-inch pieces.

It is interesting that while the English have always liked neat flower borders, they have preferred more naturalistic garden designs, while the French and Italians preferred a more orderly and formal flower garden design.

Prices for garden row markers range from $45-$125 depending on styling, completeness and design. Tailles, tallies, or labels vary in price depending on age and provenance. Labels from well-known gardens also bring in higher prices.

Generally they are priced between $35-$75.

A long-handled standing edger, 19th century, English. *Courtesy of The Sugarplum.*

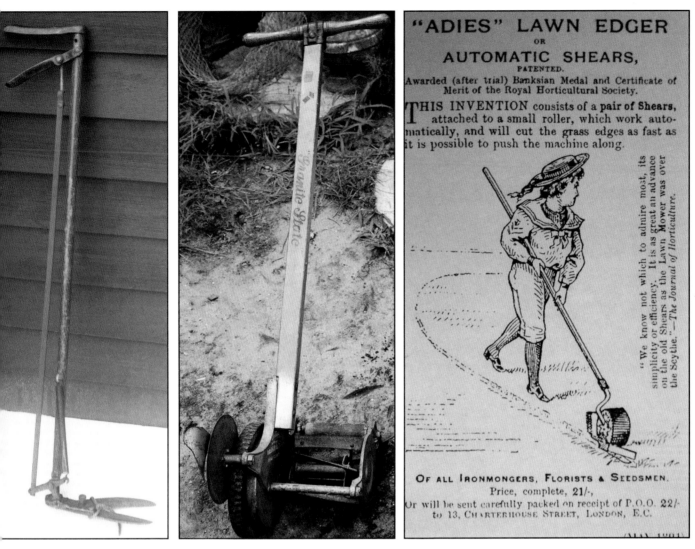

Edger   Edger.   An 1891 advertisement for a child's lawn edger.

Garden edging forms: Plain edging sells in the range of $10-15, while more
ornate edging forms range in price for $10-25.

Garden sign, $200-250, English. *Courtesy of Riverbank Antiques.*

Top right: Garden path edger, c. 1900, English. Williams & Iles & Co. made these. This is a brown rope edge form. The company also made cream colored ones. *Courtesy of the Museum of Garden History.*

Right: Terracotta garden path edgers, 1900, English, $25- 35. *Courtesy of Riverbank Antiques.*

Garden path edgers, 19th century-early 20th century, English. Roped edging forms' pricing ranges are $15-25. *Courtesy of The Sugarplum.*

Ornate cast iron edging form, English, 19th-20th century, $15-25. *Courtesy of The Sugarplum.*

Ornate cast iron edging form, English, 19th-20th century, $15-25. *Courtesy of The Sugarplum.*

Gothic shaped, garden edging form, Victorian, c. 1860. *Courtesy of Riverbank Antiques.*

Ornate edging forms, 19th-20th century, English, $20-30. *Courtesy of The Sugarplum.*

19th century, cast iron, French, $10-15. *Courtesy of Riverbank Antiques.*

Cast iron metal edgers, 19th century, English, $10. *Courtesy of Riverbank Antiques.*

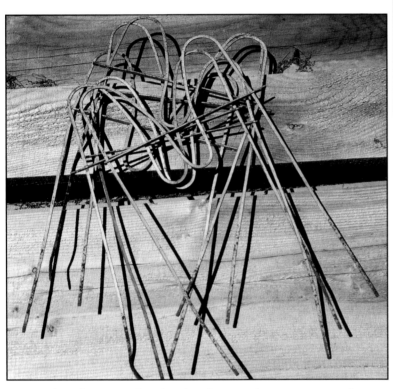

Wire edging forms, French, 19th-early 20th century, $10-15. *Courtesy of Riverbank Antiques.*

Close-up.

Wire-mesh edging, French, 19ᵗʰ-early 20ᵗʰ century, $15-20. *Courtesy of Riverbank Antiques.*

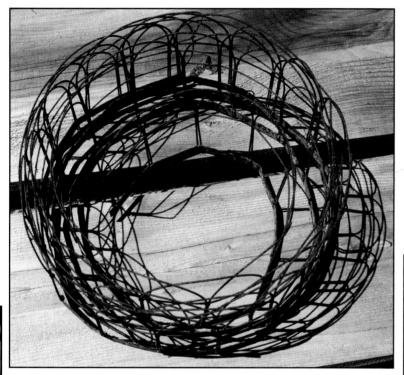

More wire mesh edging. *Courtesy of Riverbank Antiques.*

Garden row markers or garden liners were important for keeping planting in rows, maintaining property lines and laying out gardens . Today it is difficult and rare to find garden row markers that are complete. Garden row markers are priced at $50-100 depending on whether they have their twine markers and are complete.

Top right: Garden liner, 19ᵗʰ century, English. The string and markers are inside the box. $75-100. *Courtesy of the Museum of Garden History.*

Right: 20ᵗʰ century garden edging.

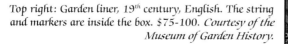

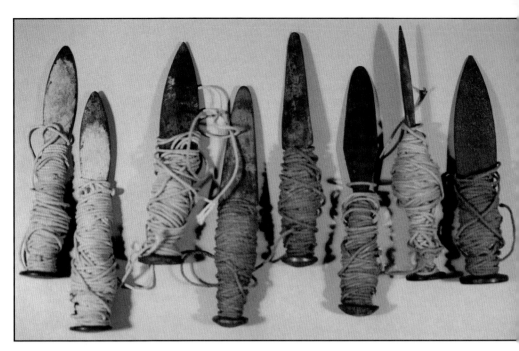

Garden lines/row markers, English, c. 1920, $30-50. *Courtesy of The Sugarplum.*

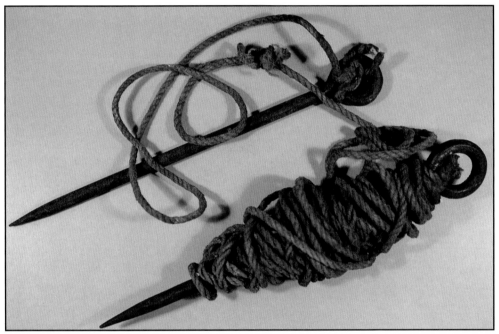

Left: Garden row marker, c. 1900, English, $45-95. *Courtesy of The Sugarplum.*

Bottom left: Garden liner or garden reel, 18th century, English. *Courtesy of the Museum of Garden History.*

Garden row marker or tallie, 19th century, English. In the 1841 *The Ladies Home Companion to the Flower Garden* advised that porcelain tallies or labels were better for pots, while lead was best, and cast iron labels were best for plants in the open ground. *Courtesy of The Sugarplum.*

Garden row marker, English, c. 1900, $45-95. *Courtesy of The Sugarplum.*

Garden reels, 19th-20th century, English, $50-65. *Courtesy of Riverbank Antiques.*

Garden row markers, English, c. 1880, $85-150. *Courtesy of The Sugarplum.*

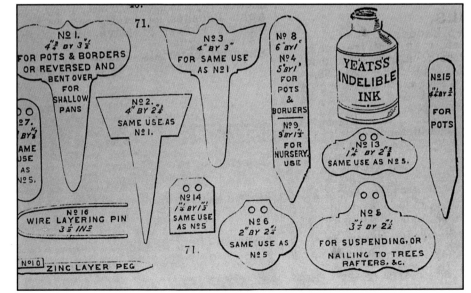

A page from a 1898 Carters tool catalog, English.

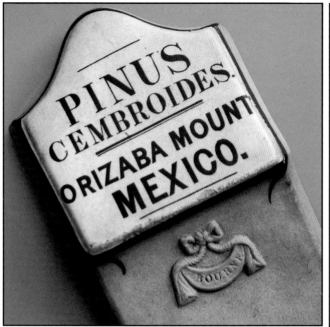

Large porcelain tallie, mid-19th century, English, manufactured by Bourne in England. This one is a tree marker. *Courtesy of the Museum of Garden History.*

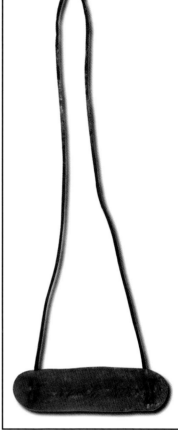

Lead and wire plant marking label, early 20th century, English. *Courtesy of The Sugarplum.*

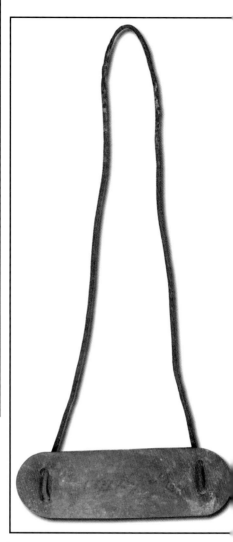

Lead and wire plant marking label, early 20th century, English, $15-25. *Courtesy of The Sugarplum.*

In the 1841 the Ladies Home Companion to the Flower Garden advised that cast iron labels were best for plants in the open ground. 19th century, English. *Courtesy of the Museum of Garden History.*

Lead plant markers, 19th century-
early 20th century, $10, French.
Courtesy of Riverbank Antiques.

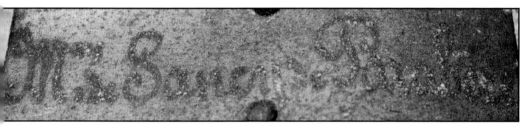

Detail

Cast iron and lead plant labels or markers, late 19th century-early 20th
century, English, $15-20. These markers either hung from wires or if it
had spikes it would be pushed into the earth. *Courtesy of the Museum
of Garden History.*

Cast iron plant marker, 20th
century, English. *Courtesy of
the Museum of Garden
History.*

Planted to commemorate the Coronation of King George VI in 1937. *Courtesy of the Museum of Garden History.*

Porcelain labels, French and English, 1930s. *Courtesy of the Museum of Garden History.* The small white oval ones (Pond's Seedling) were made in the 1930s and were used by George Fox & Sons at Roxe Vale Nursery, Cornwall, England.

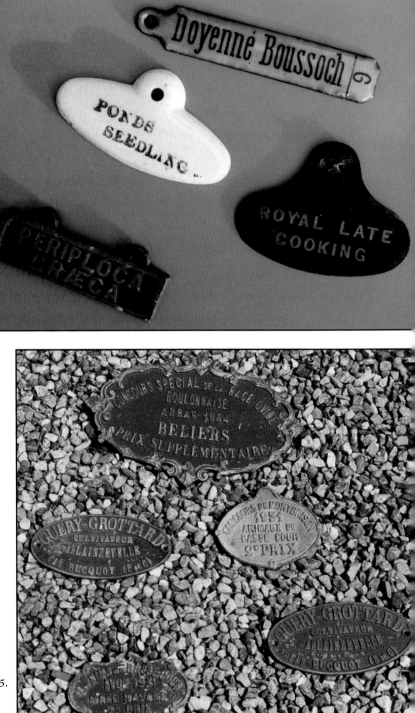

English, 20th century. *Courtesy of the Museum of Garden History.*

French, 20th century, $10-15.

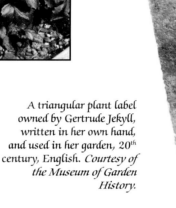

A triangular plant label owned by Gertrude Jekyll, written in her own hand, and used in her garden, 20th century, English. *Courtesy of the Museum of Garden History.*

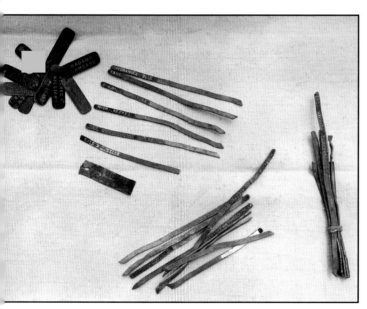

Lead plant markers, 19th century, American. *Courtesy of Riverbank Antiques.*

Close up detail. *Courtesy of the Sugarplum.*

Lead plant markers, 19th-20th century, $30-75. These lead labels come from the Chelsea Physic Garden. The Chelsea Physic Garden, a 1.6 hectares garden in Chelsea, London, was founded in 1673 by the Society of Apothecaries to demonstrate the growing of medicinal plants. From 1722 under the curatorial leadership of Philip Miller, it became one of the most famous botanic gardens in the world with more varieties of plants than any other garden. *Courtesy of The Sugarplum.*

Protecting Plants

Photo by Monika Dorman.

Forcers, Straighteners, Terracotta Pots, Melon Stands, Cloches, Hand Lights, & Greenhouses

Cloches were glass bell jars that acted as "small portable greenhouses" designed to extend the growing season by protecting young plants from sudden shifts in weather in the early spring. Cloches protected the plants by heating up the ground around the young plants and seedlings.

Glass blowers were making opaque glass cloches or plant protectors as early as the fifteenth and sixteenth centuries, but it wasn't until the nineteenth century that French gardeners introduced the use of these "handlights," "cloches," or "bell-jars" to protect their plants from weather and insects. These glass boxes came in many shapes and forms. The most popular were domed, bell jar, and pyramid shapes. In the early nineteenth century they were framed by cast-metal. Later versions were made of glass with lead frames. Later in the twentieth century zinc was used to frame the glass.

Glass had the obvious advantages of visibility and full exposure to sun. Most of the early cloches were clear glass, but due to the glass blowing process some had colors such as pink, cloudy white, blue and green. Cloches were designed for easy storage and stacked one on top of the other. The most common shape is the pyramid. The rarest form is the octagon. These cloches were durable enough to be left out in the fields. The French introduced this technique in the mid-1800s, but they didn't cross the Channel and become popular in England until the 1900s.

An interesting twentieth century variation was a "continuous cloche," a series of connecting glass cloches. A 1931 Carters catalog advertised a Chase continuous cloche. These cloches were "easy to erect, instantly portable, and perfectly rigid." They also provided adequate ventilation. These linked together with each end open, forming a continuous line of protection for the crops when the vegetables were planted in a row. Since each cloche was a manageable size, it was easy to keep adding them as needed.

Pricing forcers is complex. Simple glass forcers can be found for $20-40. Specialized ones are more expensive. Rhubarb forcers can cost $200.

Wasp traps, 19th century, English/French. A sugary substance was placed in the bottom and the traps were hung near fruit or grapes, etc. The wasps supposedly were lured into the traps to drown. These traps have also been misidentified as grape preserving bottles.
Courtesy of the Museum of Garden History.

Kale, rhubarb, celery and plant forcers, 19th century-20th century, English, $185-200. *Courtesy of Riverbank Antiques.*

Orchid forcer, 19th century-20th century, English, terracotta, $75-125. *Courtesy of Riverbank Antiques.*

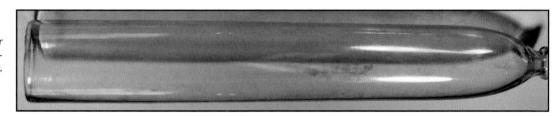

19th century glass cucumber straightener, 19th century, $200-250. *Courtesy of The Sugarplum.*

Cucumber straightener, 19th century, $200-250. The cucumber had to be pulled out gently because it was too costly to break the glass. This was a popular Victorian gardening novelty accessory. The neck of the straightener was tied by a string to a vine support and the young vegetable was placed inside and "forced" to grow straight. Most of these were pre-1914. *Courtesy of the Museum of Garden History.*

Left: crocus or saffron pot, French, c. 1950. The crocus corms were planted in the side holes. Middle and right: two sizes of orchid pots, 19ᵗʰ-20ᵗʰ century, English, terracotta. Saffron is the most expensive spice in the world. Saffron comes from crocus sativus. The stigmas of croci are picked to produce saffron. It takes about 8000-10,000 flowers to produce just 50 grams of saffron. The orchid pots provide a suitable growing environment as many orchids have aerial roots. Sometimes it is difficult tell orchid and saffron pots apart because they look so similar. *Courtesy of the Museum of Garden History.*

Another view of this orchid or saffron pot. *Courtesy of Riverbank Antiques.*

Parsley pot, c. 1975, made for Habitat stores, England for individual parsley plants to be placed in each hole. *Courtesy of the Museum of Garden History.*

Captain Bligh of *Mutiny on the Bounty* fame is buried in the garden of the Museum of Garden History.

Orchid pot, terracotta, 19th century, England. *Courtesy of the Museum of Garden History.*

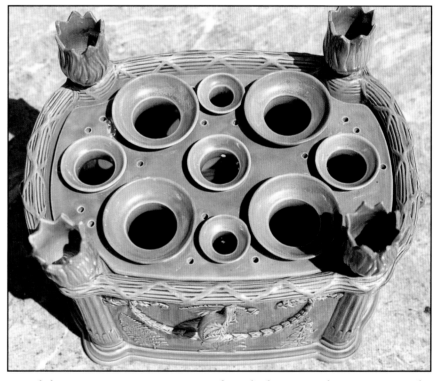

English crocus pot, c. 1720-50. *Courtesy of Riverbank Antiques.* This very rare piece of Bramfeld china is very unusual. Wedgwood made its own china version of a crocus pot in 1790, but its version was plainer and square with holes in the top and trim that simulated bamboo.

Celery forcer, 19th century, terracotta, $150-200.
Courtesy of the Museum of Garden History.

Rhubarb, Kale pots, 19th century-20th century, terracotta, $185-200, English.

Kale and rhubarb forcers and melon stands. *Courtesy of Riverbank Antiques.*

Sea kale forcer.

Asparagus forcers, French, c. 1900, $65-75. *Courtesy of Riverbank Antiques.*

Seedling tray, ceramic, English, 19th-20th century. *Courtesy of Riverbank Antiques.*

Sea kale (Crambe maritima) forcer, decorated terracotta, c. 1855, made by G. Harris and Company for forcing sea kale, English, 19th century, $85-100. The lid is missing and probably would have been domed. It is unusual to find such nice painted decoration. Sea kale forcers were 16 inches x 16 inches deep or 13 inches x 13 inches deep. Rhubarb forcers were taller and were 16 inches x 24 inches deep. *Courtesy of Riverbank Antiques.*

Melon stands, 19th century, $35-50, French. *Courtesy of Riverbank Antiques.*

Melon pot, 19th century, French. *Courtesy of Riverbank Antiques.*

91

Melon pots, English 19th century. *Courtesy of the Museum of Garden History.*

Baked clay pots have been used for plants since the Tudor period.

No. 98
No. 98, 7½ in., per doz., $6.00

An illustration from Parker & Wood , a 19th century English agricultural store. *Courtesy of Hinck and Wall.*

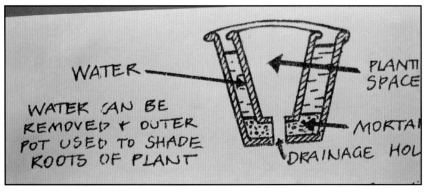

WATER

WATER CAN BE REMOVED & OUTER POT USED TO SHADE ROOTS OF PLANT

PLANTI SPACE

MORTA

DRAINAGE HOL

Drawing of a double pot. These pots were used for plants which required constant moisture. *Drawing by Philip Norman.*

Catalog rendition of a double pot.

This pot was used by Queen Elizabeth II's gardener and is marked with her initials, Elizabeth Regina, c. 1953. *Courtesy of the Museum of Garden History.*

Hanging wall pot, English, made by Sankey, c. 1890, $60-125. This is a very rare hanging pot. *Courtesy of The Sugarplum.*

Bulb bowl, English, c. 1900. Potters often decorated terracotta bowls and pots with scalloped trims, leaves, and other designs. $30-35. *Courtesy of The Sugarplum.*

English, 20th century, terracotta pots manufactured by Sankeys. $30-40. *Courtesy of Riverbank Antiques.*

Detail.

Galvanized tin and aluminum pails, 20th century, American. *Courtesy of Larkspur Farms.*

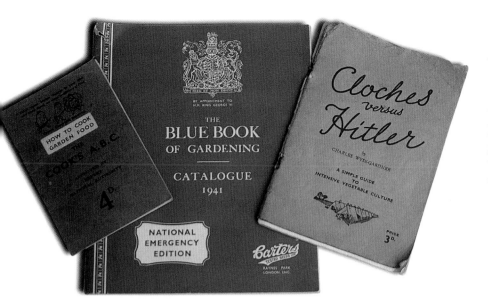

Since cloches prolonged and extended the growing season and a garden's productivity, during the 1940s the English War Ministry developed a program called "cloches for Hitler," which encouraged home gardeners to produce more food in their gardens by using glass cloches to protect the plants and get them off to an early start, therefore increasing the homefront's food production.

World War II English propaganda, $35-45. "Cloches for Hitler" became a popular rallying cry for English "Victory" gardeners who were encouraged to use cloches to grow more food and vegetables to feed the home front. Cloches encouraged and stimulated growth. *Courtesy of the Museum of Garden History.*

Pyramid shaped cloche. *Courtesy of the Museum of Garden History.*

Cloches. *Courtesy of the Museum of Garden History.*

Gardeners also used terracotta pots, terracotta forcers, and glass straighteners to create more attractive vegetables. Gardeners placed cylindrical "chimney pots" over the plants to improve color, shape and taste. "Forcers" or bell shaped terracotta pots with lids were placed over asparagus, celery, sea kale, parsley, and lettuce plants to induce them to "blanche" which, in theory, would produce a better taste. Glass forcers were intended to get the plants off to a better start and protect young plants from variations and aberrations of unusual climate.

Glass/lead cloche, English/French, 1870, $150-175. This particular shape was designed with sloped sides for maximum sun exposure and ventilation. Sloped sides also enabled the water to run off. *Courtesy of Riverbank Antiques.*

Another version

Cloche, 19th century, French.

The larger cloche is French, c. 1870-90, $225-275. The smaller ones are handlights, made by Chase, England, 1920-30, $65-75. *Courtesy of Riverbank Antiques.*

Some of the most common glass straighteners were designed to make cucumbers grow straighter. The cucumber had to be pulled out of the glass tube gently because it was too costly to break the glass. Most simple glass forcers today are valued in the range of $20-$40. Well preserved ones can range upwards of $200-$250. Terracotta forcers are worth more in the $150-$400 range depending on size. Forcers, with their original lids, are rare and since few have survived intact, they command higher prices. Victorian forcers are valued at between $200-$300.

Baked clay pots have been used as planting containers as early as the Tudor period. The sloped-sided shape came from utilitarian needs. They were easy to stack, store, and allowed for a fuller plant growth. During the Victorian period, potters began to embellish these pots with scalloped edges, and leaf and scroll designs.

Photo by Monika Dorman.

Photo by Monika Dorman.

A 1833 *Gardener's Magazine* illustration showed a double pot which was designed for marsh plants or for shading the roots of tender plants or other plants requiring constant moisture. Later in Victorian times, these pots were used for rooting cuttings in soil placed between the two pots, with water in the middle pot when needed and a bell glass placed over the top to provide a "beneficial climate."

Nineteenth century potters made double pots with a bulbous decorative outer pot and a plainer pot placed inside. A 1900 catalog recommended this kind of pot for ferns since it "obviated the use of an unsightly earthenware flowerpot" inside.

In order to prevent melons from rotting in the fields, the melons were often placed on terracotta melon stands or melon boxes. Melon stands have often been confused with forms for edging borders.

Richard Sankey and Son, Ltd., Bulwell, Nottingham are the most famous producers of flowerpots in Britain. The company was founded in 1855 at Bulwell and the flowerpots are usually marked with their name just beneath the rim. Sankey halted production of clay pots in the 1980s and now produces plastic. While the Edwardians used some machine-manufactured pots, terracotta pots were still being hand-thrown up to the beginning of World War II.

Pots vary in price depending on size, design and details. Sankeys is a well-known manufacturer and the company produced pots of many sizes from very small ones for seedlings to larger ones for fuller plants. Small-sized pots are priced at $2. Larger pots can be priced upwards to $50. There are many styles of pots. A particularly popular pot was designed with a terracotta drape.

19th century-early 20th century, American, greenhouse heating unit.

Courtesy of Gramercy Tavern, Roberta BenDavid Designs.

Insects and Garden Pests

Glass wasp traps, 19th century, French. Courtesy of the Museum of Garden History.

Sprayers, Flytraps, Traps, & Beekeeping

Insects, small rodents and birds have always been the gardener's nemesis, and man has gone to exotic means to protect his harvest. One of the simplest methods was to drape cloth, rattan coverings or gauze bags to protect crops, particularly fruit and berries.

However, the most efficient and proven means against insects were poisons, necessitating sprayers, bellows, puffers, and chemical insecticides. Some of the earliest poisons were a mixture of tobacco leaves mixed with iron sulfate and sulfur, and what would become one of the most efficient, arsenic. During the late nineteenth and early twentieth centuries, gardeners used arsenic both in their insecticide puffers and sprayers and their mole and rodent traps. Today it is not uncommon to find remnants of arsenic inside the bellows of antique sprayers.

Photo by Monika Dorman.

Photo by Monika Dorman.

Victorian birdcages. *Courtesy of Riverbank Antiques.*

Pollinating bee boxes. *Courtesy of After Math Acres, LaConner, Washington.*

Photo by Monika Dorman.

Victorian birdcage. *Courtesy of Riverbank Antiques.*

Arsenic got results and it is interesting to note that the use of arsenic was so widespread among English country gardeners that the popular English mystery writer Agatha Christie often found her murder weapon, arsenic, in the potting shed of country estates.

Gardeners also designed many unique and often makeshift varieties of repellents designed to scare away birds. Victorian gardeners designed bird scarers made out of twigs, noisemakers, sheet metal cats, old fashioned scarecrows, and field apparatuses of bells and rattles. One of their most ingenious devices was a web-like barrier of twigs and strings that was laid across the crop.

Fruit growers hung glass fly and wasp traps from trees and bushes. A sugary substance was placed in the bottom of these hanging glass jars and the wasps were lured inside to drown. Most fly and wasp traps were French.

Pricing flytraps depends on condition, color, and quality of the glass. Clear glass traps are the commonest to find and the cheapest, and generally range in price from $25-$80. Colored glass such as amethyst, cloudy white, blue or pink, bring much higher prices. Amethyst glass traps bring in hundreds of dollars and are very rare.

In addition, gardeners used specially shaped glass bottles as fish traps to catch fish and move them into ponds, hanging tin pitchers to give their pigeons water, and maintained aviaries to keep exotic bird specimens.

Beekeeping was also important to gardeners. Bees had two functions to pollinate flowers and produce honey.

Fences have always been one of the best defenses against bigger garden pests, both human and animal.

Insecticide puffers. Left: marked Acme 22 patent probably English c. 1910 used as a bellows effect to puff insecticide powder on infected plants. Middle: marked Vicat Soufflet Parisien , French, c. 1920; Right: Unmarked, possibly French, c. 1920. When the lid was depressed, it produced a puff of insecticide dust. Courtesy of the Museum of Garden History.

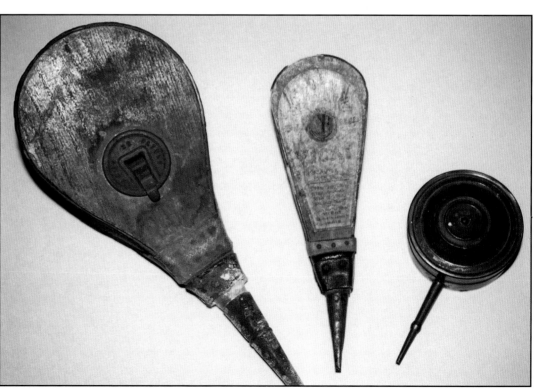

Insecticide sprayers and water pumps, 19th-early
20th century, English, *Courtesy of the Museum of
Garden History.*

A bellows sprayer, 19th century, English. *Courtesy of the
Museum of Garden History.*

Garden and field sprayers, American,
late 19th century-early 20th century.
Courtesy of Tillinghast Seeds.

Non-poisonous
Abol Insecticide

Green and Black Fly, Woolly Aphis, etc., Mildew
on Roses and other plants, are easily and surely exter-
minated by means of Abol Non-poisonous Insecticide. Abol
has been the leading plant wash for many years, being
perfectly safe to use on all flowers fruits and vegetables.

It is clean and wholesome to handle, has no unpleasant smell and
will not damage paintwork.

Used in the Royal Gardens.

An interesting and helpful treatise on Garden Pests, will be sent to anyone, gratis
and post free.

Now supplied in square tins : ½-pt. 1/4 ; pt. 2 2 ; qt. 3/4 ; ½-gall. 5/3 ; gall. 9/6

The Syringe with
the Perfect Spray

Abol Patent Syringes give a fine strong spray, which may be varied in density,
from very fine, to medium or coarse, as desired. They are specially recommended by
the National Rose Society, and many have been in use for over twenty years.

No. 4 (1 × 14) 16/4   Bend, for directing spray
No. 5 (1 × 20) 21/-   to undersides of leaves,
No. 6 (1½× 20) 26/-   not included, but 1/6 extra

Of all Nurserymen, Seedsmen, Ironmongers, etc.   Sole Proprietors and Mnfrs.,
Abol Limited, 54, Belring, Paddock Wood, Kent.

A 19th century English advertisement for
a child-sized insect sprayer.

Hand sprayer used for spraying roses or fruit trees, early 20th, English. This Carters Ideal Sprayer was used by the gardeners of the Royal Botanic Gardens at Kew and was awarded three gold medals for merit in 1923. It came with three sized sprays-one pint, two pints, and 3 pints. The two pint sprayer, when full, gave out more than 100 sprays and sprayed up to 25 to 30 feet high. It was advertised as ideal for spraying fruit trees. *Courtesy of Riverbank Antiques.*

A page from a 1926 Carters Garden tool catalog, English.

Pricing for flytraps depend on the color and quality of the glass. Clear glass traps are the commonest to find and the cheapest and generally range in price from $25-60. Colored glass such as amethyst, cloudy white, blue or pink tinges bring in much higher prices. Amethyst glass traps bring in hundreds of dollars and are very rare.

Wasp traps, 19th century, French. These traps were used in apple orchards. The fish traps, 19th century, English, $25-80, were used to catch fish for fishponds. *Courtesy of Riverbank Antiques.*

Fly traps for fruit trees, 20th century, French, $35-45. *Courtesy of Riverbank Antiques.*

Fly-wasp trap, French, 1850-70, $125. *Courtesy of Riverbank Antiques.*

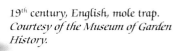

19th century, English, mole trap. *Courtesy of the Museum of Garden History.*

Fish carriers, 19th century, English, $60-75. *Courtesy of Riverbank Antiques.*

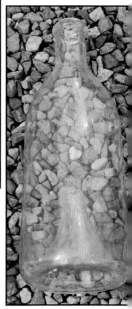

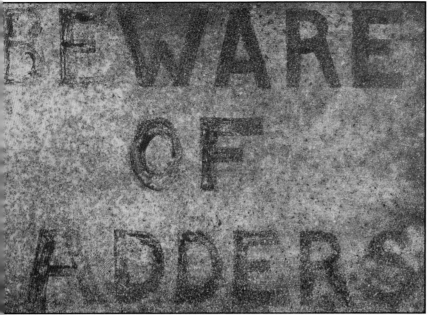

19th century garden sign, English, $60-90. Garden signs such as this "beware of adders" are very collectible and desirable. It is rare to find one in such nice condition. *Courtesy of The Sugarplum.*

English, early 20th century, $35. *Courtesy of The Sugarplum.*

Bee swarmers/movers, English, 19th century, $300-350 a pair. The queen bee was placed inside to attract the worker bees. *Courtesy of Riverbank Antiques.*

Vintage Edwardian postcard of beehives and bee boxes, c. 1900, English, $15-25. Postcards of such unusual activities as beekeeping command higher prices since they are rarer. *Courtesy of the Museum of Garden History.*

An award from the British BeeKeepers Association, $75-130. *Courtesy of The Sugarplum.*

Detail.

Beeboxes, wood, 20th century, American. *Courtesy of Riverbank Antiques.*

Bee-smoker, 19th century, American, $30-60 depending on condition. *Courtesy of Riverbank Antiques.*

Detail.

Beekeeper's hat and mask, $75-90. *Courtesy of Riverbank Antiques.*

Pigeon waterer, French, c. 1920, $125-150. *Courtesy of Riverbank Antiques.*

Garden art made by Mary Taylor, Rosebar, LaConner, Washington.

Victorian birdcages. *Courtesy of Riverbank Antiques.*

Hanging wasp or insect trap, 19th century, French, $75-90. *Courtesy of Riverbank Antiques.*

Detail.

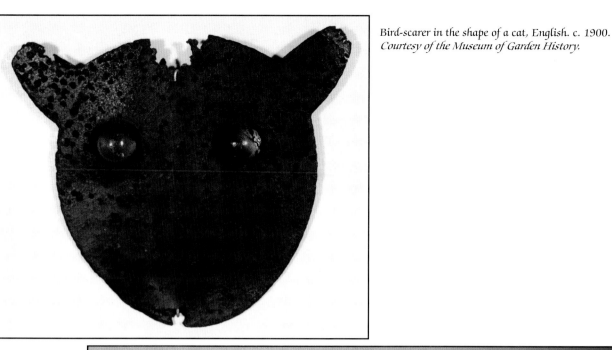

Bird-scarer in the shape of a cat, English. c. 1900. *Courtesy of the Museum of Garden History.*

Large black and white cat, bird-scarer, c. 1900, English, sheet metal. *Courtesy of the Museum of Garden History.*

Bird-scarer. This is a late 19th century English noisemaker to scare away birds from fields and gardens. The shape is similar to noisemakers used in vaudeville to hiss and boo the villains and the groggers used by Jews during the spring festival of Purim to drown out the name of the anti-Semitic villain, Haman. *Courtesy of the Museum of Garden History.*

Twigs and string bird-scarer, late 19th century, English. A web-like barrier laid across the top of seed or flowerbeds to protect them from birds and insects. *Courtesy of the Museum of Garden History.*

111

Photo by Monika Dorman.

Garden bell, 19ᵗʰ –20ᵗʰ century, American. *Courtesy of Riverbank Antiques.*

Watering

Watering Cans

Water is essential for a gardener and carrying water to a garden demanded ingenuity. The earliest water carriers were animal skin and leather containers. The Greeks and Romans used terracotta and clay. In the sixteenth century, earthenware pottery was introduced.

The thumb pot was the first watering pot as we know it. It was the invention of a sixteenth century monk, Jethro Hull, who used to sprinkle water on his plants through his outstretched fingers. He made history when he accidentally dropped a clay pot into a tub of water and then put his finger over the hole, created suction, which when released, forced the water to pour out through the holes. This discovery revolutionized gardening. By the seventeenth century, gardeners were using earthenware watering pots with perforated pouring holes.

The name "watering can" dates from the mid-eighteenth century. By then gardeners were using portable watering pots of all kinds. The French were making copper pots and the Dutch manufactured brass pots, while the Italians continued to make earthenware containers. By the early nineteenth century, gardeners began to use zinc and tin-coated watering pots.

Like other garden tools, watering cans evolved from familiar household shapes: pails, pitchers, and pots. Their pouring spouts also evolved from functional needs. Gardeners demanded different forms to maneuver among the plants and the plantings. One of the best adaptations was the conservatory can with its long nosed spout. Long spouts were designed for hard to reach gardening needs such as window boxes, the ends of flowerbeds, and conservatory shelves.

Good watering techniques sprinkled water on plants rather than inundating them with floods of water and soon gardeners found that "roses" or rosettes regulated the flow. Rosettes came in different shapes and sizes. The English particularly liked pointed roses.

Nowhere does form follow function as well as it does with watering can handles. The English preferred cans with two separate handles, one for carrying and handling, and the other for pouring. The French preferred one all purpose handle.

In 1886 John Haws of Clapton in London patented his first watering can designed to have perfect balance no matter how much water was in the can. His company also produced other watering devices- i.e watercarts, sprayers, etc. Today the company still produces traditional Victorian/Edwardian designs, as well as plastic versions and also indoor planters in copper and plastic. Of all the Haws modifications, the watering can with a crown top was its most popular.

Photo by Monika Dorman.

Watering cans are among the most popular garden tool collectibles and canny dealers know the advantage of waxing and cleaning up old rusted cans to get better value. Color is also an important consideration. Red is one of the most popular and most common colors since red was the cheapest color available. Blue and green were other popular colors. Nineteenth century companies advertised "japanned red" watering cans. Today gardeners seem to like yellow. The advantage of bright colors is visibility, since gardeners have the tendency to drop their tools in the garden as they work.

It is easy to date watering cans by material, shape, spout, and handle. Early nineteenth century cans had wire struts to support the pouring spout. By the twentieth century fewer cans had supporting struts. Before mass production, there was a great variety in the thickness of handles. Nineteenth and early twentieth century gardening manufacturers produced cans with handles of varied thickness to accommodate individual gardeners' hands.

Courtesy of Larkspur Farms

Bottom: a 1990 reproduction of a 17th century earthenware original which may have been made in Sussex. Top: a 20th century two-handle watering can.

Metal and galvanized watering cans are very popular among collectors, and their prices range from $45-$150 depending on condition, styling and pouring spouts. Missing rosettes are not a problem since they can be replaced. Children's watering cans are worth double their adult-sized counterparts and bring in prices upwards of $125.

Earthenware pots are very desirable and bring in extremely high prices. Authentic Tudor period pots have brought prices as high as $4000 at auction. Early seventeenth century and eighteenth century pots can bring in hundreds of dollars. Collectors particularly like shapes. Paint also adds to value and collector interest. Watering cans are particularly collectible because of their size and their sculptural quality. Unlike tools, they have a presence and make a decorative statement on a porch or in a garden.

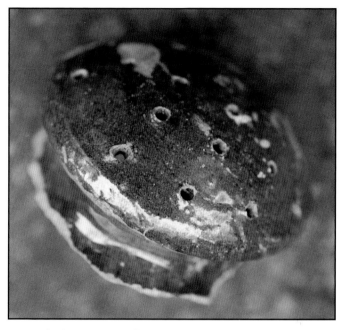

Detail. This rosette was found during an archeological expedition in northern England. It dates from the 17th century.

Vintage post card showing three gardeners standing in the conservatory holding watering cans by their spouts, Edwardian, English, $5-10. *Courtesy of the Museum of Garden History.*

American, French and Danish watering cans, 20th century (mid 1940s-1950s) $65-85 each. Red is one of the most popular colors of watering cans since red pigment was the most available and cheapest color available. Other popular colors were blue and green.

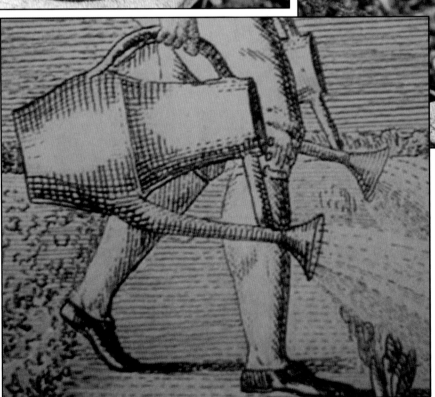

An early 19th century copper French watering can.

Watering can, 20th century, French.

Two English two-handle conservatory watering cans and a French 20th century watering can, $85-100. Courtesy of The Sugarplum.

Two conservatory styled watering cans. Courtesy of the Museum of Garden History.

Photo by Monika Dorman.

Conservatory watering can, 19th-20th century, English, $45-60.
Courtesy of Riverbank Antiques.

Detail.

Conservatory watering can, painted, French, 19th century. Conservatory cans range in price from $90-150. Ordinary painted cans range in price from $45-60. *Courtesy of The Sugarplum.*

Conservatory watering can, English, 19th-20th century, $90-150. *Courtesy of The Sugarplum.*

Detail. Haws was a well-known manufacturer of English watering cans. The company was particularly well known for its watering can innovations. In 1886 John Haws of Clapton in London patented their first watering can–designed to have perfect balance no matter how much water was in the can. The company produced watering cans and other watering devices, i.e watercarts, sprayers etc. Today the company still produces their traditional Victorian/ Edwardian designs, as well as plastic versions and also indoor planters in copper and plastic.

English-style watering can, 19th century, $45-65. *Courtesy of The Sugarplum.*

Thumb watering pot, reproduction, Tudor-style, $75. A 16th century original sold a few years ago in England for $4000 at auction. *Courtesy of the Museum of Garden History.*

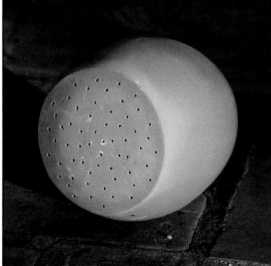

Detail of sprinkler.

Terracotta sprinkler.

Another view.

English-style watering can, French, 19th century. *Courtesy of The Sugarplum.*

English-style handle watering can. *Courtesy of The Sugarplum.*

120

20th century American watering cans. *Courtesy of Larkspur Farms.*

20th century, American. *Courtesy of Larkspur Farms.*

Watering can, c. 1900, American. Note the unusual handle.

Watering can, English, 19th-early 20th century. This is an unusual painted watering can. The body is green, the rosette is red. *Courtesy of Larkspur Farms.*

121

Watering cans, blue, 19th century, French, $50-200 depending on condition and size. *Courtesy of The Sugarplum.*

Conservatory watering cans, English, 20th century. *Courtesy of Larkspur Farms.*

Notice the struts supporting the spout of this watering can. *Courtesy of the Museum of Garden History.*

Watering cans like other garden tools are designed for specific purposes. *Courtesy of Larkspur Farms.*

Child-sized watering can, 20th century, American, $125-150.

Two conservatory watering cans, English, 20th century, $45-65. *Courtesy of Riverbank Antiques.*

Watering can rosettes, $10.

123

Miniature brass toy watering can.

Galvanized tin watering pitcher.

Watering pitcher, 20th century, French.

Watering can, early 20th century, painted enamel, child-sized, $130-150. Children's watering cans are now very desirable and bring in higher prices than adult-sized watering cans because they are rarer. Too many of these toys were discarded and thus they are often difficult to find. In addition garden tools are just becoming collectible, whereas vintage toys have always been collectible and coveted by toy collectors and thus the market is already established. *Courtesy of Riverbank Antiques.*

Child's watering can, English, 20th century, $125-150.
Courtesy of the Museum of Garden History.

Miniature watering can, 19th century. *Courtesy of the Sugarplum.*

Watering can, 20th century, painted yellow.

Water Carts

By the mid-nineteenth century rolling water carts were introduced and found in most large country estates. The early carts could hold up to sixty gallons of water, but by the early twentieth century they were more compact and less bulky. "Dolly tubs" or galvanized wash tubs and barrels, although, not originally intended for garden use, today are used by gardeners and placed in gardens to catch and store rainwater. These tubs were made in England from 1880-1930 and have been called French rain barrels although they never came from France. Their prices range from $75-$200.

Sprinklers & Hose Reels

The nineteenth century invention of vulcanized rubber lead to the creation and manufacture of hoses which were a breakthrough in gardening efficiency. By 1860, wooden hose racks became popular and soon became a gardener's second hand. These "T" shaped hose reels were staked into the garden and then the hose was pulled by the gardener and used at will. The hose reel was designed to hold garden hose, as well as provide a space to stack garden hoses easily both in potting sheds, on lawns and in the garden. Today these Victorian hose/stakes are valued in the range of $25-$50.

Larger water carts are less desirable to collectors because they present an obvious storage problem, and since they are usually rusted and well worn, they are not very attractive. Their value is in the $85-$150 range.

Watering trough, 20th century, American, cast iron.

Water trough, 19th century, English. Note that this is a more intricate design.

Detail

Japanese styled water cistern, Golden Gate Park, San Francisco, California.

Water pails, 20th century, American, galvanized tin.

Water tank, 19th century, English. *Courtesy of Riverbank Antiques.*

127

Detail of the bottom of previous page bottom right.

A page from a 1953 Louis Ford catalog.

Watercart, c. 1900, English. Gardeners would wheel this cart into the gardens and place it where gardeners could use it to fill their watering cans. *Courtesy of Riverbank Antiques.*

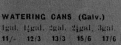

Water sprayer cart, Victorian. *Courtesy of the Museum of Garden History.*

Water or fertilizer pump, English, c. 1880, $90-100.
Courtesy of Riverbank Antiques.

Dolly tubs or wash tubs, English, 20th century, $ 75-200. Dolly tubs were wash tubs made in England from 1880-1930s. Sometimes they are called French rain barrels but they are not from France. *Courtesy of The Sugarplum.*

Often gardeners caught rainwater in these "dolly tubs" to gather water for their watering cans.

Water sprinkler heads, early 20th century. *Courtesy of the Museum of Garden History.*

Water sprinklers, 20th century c.1930-1950s, $30-45. *Courtesy of Riverbank Antiques.*

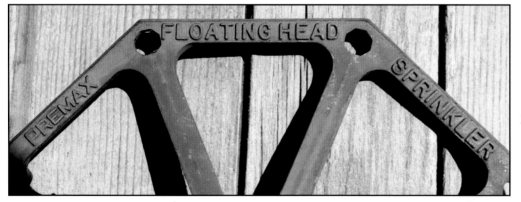

Detail.

Detail.

Water sprinkler, 20th century, American, miniature.

Miniature water sprinkler, 20th century, American.

Hose reel, American, 1930-1940, $65-75. *Courtesy of Riverbank Antiques.*

Hose and water pump, 19th century, American. *Courtesy of Riverbank Antiques.*

Water pump, 20th century, American, miniature. *Courtesy of Barbara Israel Garden Antiques.*

This gadget is a Victorian hose guard. The stake was plunged into the garden with the hose attached, and then the hose was pulled out at will, $25. *Courtesy of The Sugarplum.*

Hose reels are designed to hold and carry garden hoses. Usually they are compact so that the hoses can be easily stacked. Hose reel or hose winder, 19th century, American. *Courtesy of Riverbank Antiques.*

Hose reel, American, 1910, $95-100. *Courtesy of Riverbank Antiques.*

Pruning and Trimming

Photo by Monika Dorman.

Saws, Pruners, Secateurs, Scissors, Billhooks, Clippers, Edgers, Multi-cutters & Topiary Forms

As early as 1706, French gardener Francis Gentil wrote that he used a saw "for cutting branches which can't be lopped with a knife." Before pruners were invented in the 1800s, saws were essential to keep gardens tidy and under control.

The earliest saws were metal strips that were serrated into teeth. These serrated blades were encased in wooden frames or bows so that the blade wouldn't twist. The frames came in varying sizes depending on the task or the user. In the 1850s manufacturers began to make wider sheets of metal and saws became more manageable. One of the most interesting adaptations was a saw encased in the handle of a walking stick.

Pruning and trimming plants guarantees fuller plantings, and the variety of knives, saws, clippers, and trimmers are extraordinary. Nineteenth century gardening inventories list gooseberry knives, asparagus knives, rose pruners, propagating scissors, vine scissors, weed slashers, billhooks, budding knives, and botanists knives.

Gardening scissors and pruning knives developed as variations of ordinary barber shears, scissors, and household knives. Gardeners needed sharp, easy to grip instruments to clip, control, and train their plants.

Billhooks have always been the most essential and adaptable gardening tool. These all-purpose cutting knives have been in use since Roman times.

During the Victorian age, English gardeners delighted in creating manicured topiaries, mazes, labyrinths, hedges, and bushes. Maintaining these structures required a variety of hand-held hedge-trimming tools. Until they were replaced by electric trimmers in the 1950s, a variety of multicut, slide action cutters were used by gardeners. Since topiaries and hedges were of different heights, they required specific cutting and sliding movements. Manufacturers responded by creating small compact trimmers, larger more expansive slide actions, single-hand operated trimmers and two-handed trimmers. Each trimmer was designed for a specific purpose and a specific type of trim.

It is difficult to price these tools as collectibles since many of these tools are still in use. Antique trimmers are priced between $60-$90. Intricate mechanisms add value.

Folding knives were first made in the eighteenth century for convenience and safety. Some of the best examples were made by William Rodgers and Thomas Turner, both of Sheffield, England.

Secateurs were developed by the French to help prune their grapevines and were copied from everyday barber utensils such as scissors, shears, and ordinary cutting knives. As knife makers customized the blades and sliding mechanisms, the knife heads became more menacing and savage looking. Soon these knives were called "parrot heads" because they resembled a parrot beak. Although the Wilkinson Sword company made secateurs and gardening knives, the best ones were made by the French.

The following secateurs (French) and pruners (English) are from the collection of the Museum of Gar-

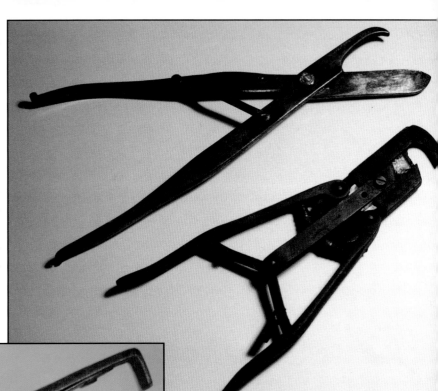

Top: Sliding action by Mosely & Son, England, c. 1900. Bottom: sliding action stamped Wynn Timmins, English, c. 1910.

Secateur, French, c. 1850, probably for vineyard work.

den History. Since the French were more interested in pruning their grape vines and fruit trees, most secateurs are of French manufacture. However, while the English copied the French, they also manufactured their own knives. The Americans preferred the European versions, but also manufactured their own.

Top: Secateur, late 19th century, French. Bottom: probably French c. 1910

Top: Auberts double action cutting secateurs, c. 1910, French. Bottom: Parrot beak secateurs, c. 1900 French.

Secateur, sliding-action pruners, Wilkinson, Sword (Greers knife cut) England, c. 1920.

Secateur, Rolcut, English, c. 1930.

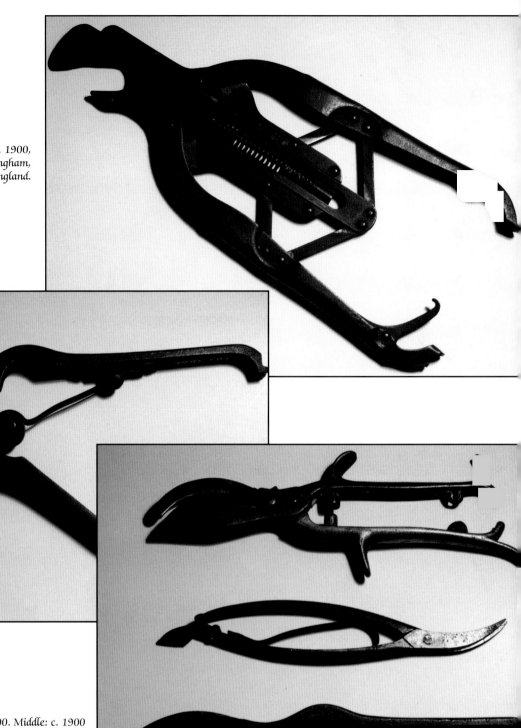

Barrows patent pruner, c. 1900, English, made in Birmingham, England.

Secateur, French, late 19th century.

Top: spring missing, English, c. 1900. Middle: c. 1900 English or French. Bottom: French c. 1910.

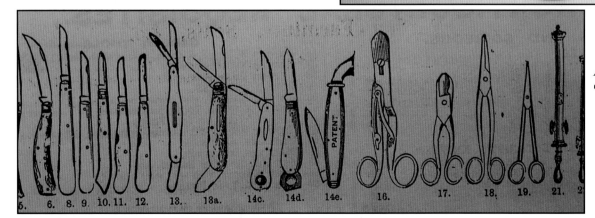

A page from a 1898 Carters tool catalog, English.

5.   6.   8.   9.   10. 11.   12.   13.   13a.   14c.   14d.   14e.   16.   17.   18.   19.   21.

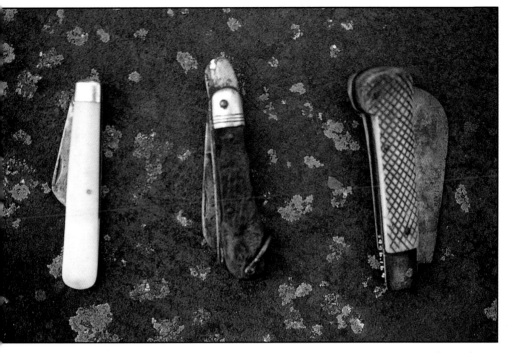

Pruning or gardener's knives.
*Courtesy of the Museum of
Garden History.*

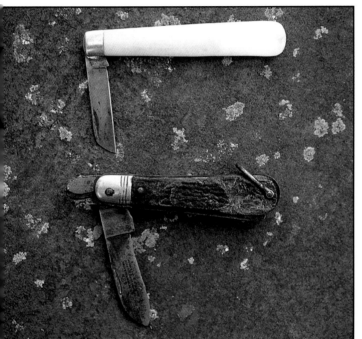

Pruning or gardener's knives.
*Courtesy of the Museum of
Garden History.*

Although the French
made the most popular
pruning gardening
knives, the English
company, Wilkinson
Sword made excellent
pruning knives. *Courtesy
of the Museum of
Garden History.*

Left: Gardener's
pruning knife, carved
bone handle, leather
sheath, c.1900,
English. Leather sheath
had belt loop for
carrying. *Courtesy of
the Museum of Garden
History.*

Right: Detail. Note the
gardener on this
handle. *Courtesy of the
Museum of Garden
History.*

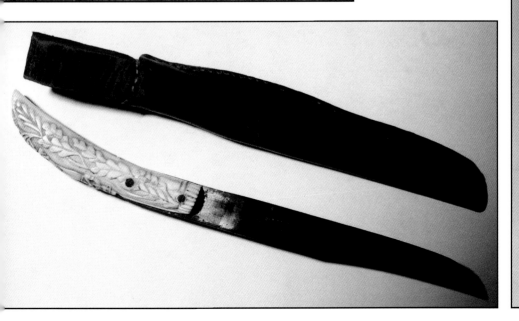

137

Folding pruning saw/knife, c. 1900, English, $40-75. Saws are differentiated from knives by their serrated blades. Folding knives were first invented in the 1700s for safety reasons. *Courtesy of The Sugarplum.*

Hand shears, English or French, early 18th century. *Courtesy of the Museum of Garden History.*

Garden shears, c. 1950, English, red painted. *Courtesy of the Museum of Garden History.*

Garden shears, Grass trimmers, 19th-early 20th century, American, $20-35. *Courtesy of Riverbank Antiques.*

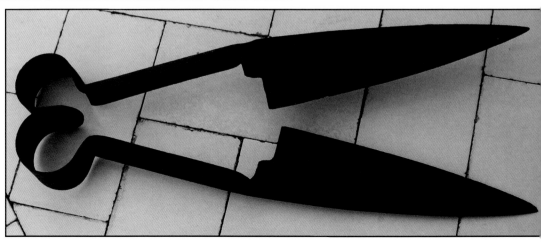

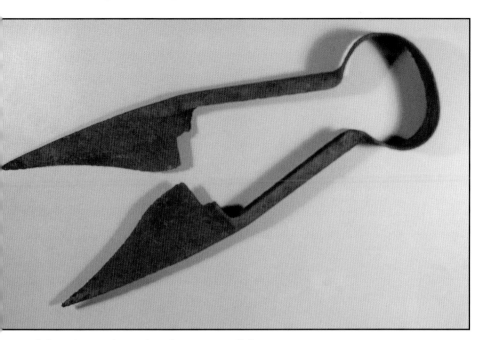

Hand shears (grass trimmers), 19th century, English, two prongs $60-85. *Courtesy of The Sugarplum.*

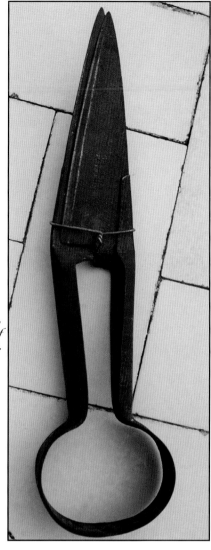

Hand shears, 19th century, American, "grasshopper," $45-60. *Courtesy of Riverbank Antiques.*

Detail.

Hand shears, 19th-20th century, American, $45-75. *Courtesy of Riverbank Antiques.*

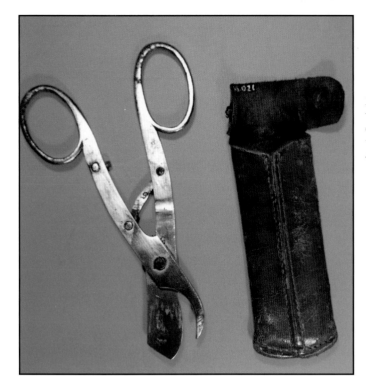

Pruning shears with leather sheath, c. 1900, English, made by Saynor, Cooke & Ridal, England. These were advertised as useful for pruning roses and bushes. Note that these scissors resemble the parrot beak of the larger secateurs. *Courtesy of the Museum of Garden History.*

Small garden scissors, c. 1900, English. *Courtesy of the Museum of Garden History.*

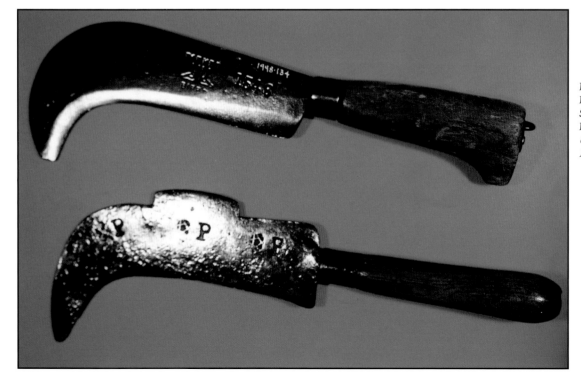

Billhooks: Top: Stamped "Parkes Biped," English, c. 1900. Bottom: Stamped Nash, English, c. 1930. Designed to be used for hedging. *Courtesy of the Museum of Garden History.*

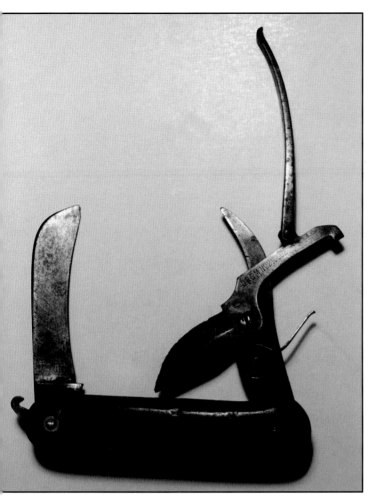

Knife, c. 1900. Made in Germany. This knife is reminiscent of the Swiss Army knife designs. Folding knives were first invented in the 1700s for safety reasons. *Courtesy of the Museum of Garden History.*

19th century, English. *Courtesy of the Museum of Garden History.*

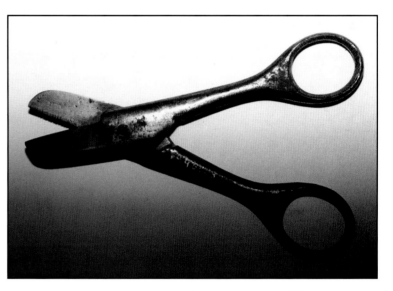

Notice the compact size of these pruners. *Courtesy of the Museum of Garden History.*

A page from a 1909 William Wood & Son garden tool catalog.

Billhook, late 18th century, English or French. *Courtesy of the Museum of Garden History.*

Weed hoe (billhook), $45-60. *Courtesy of Riverbank Antiques.*

The following are from the collection of the Museum of Garden History.

Spong garden hedge trimmer, c. 1910, with nine teeth arranged in a semicircular position, English.

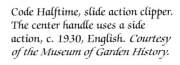

Code Halftime, slide action clipper. The center handle uses a side action, c. 1930, English. *Courtesy of the Museum of Garden History.*

Multi-cut trimmers, early 20th century, English. *Courtesy of the Museum of Garden History.*

Sliding mechanism multi-cut trimmers, early 20th century, English. *Courtesy of the Museum of Garden History.*

A page from a 1903 Louis Ford garden tool catalog.

Multi-cut trimmers, early 20th century, English. *Courtesy of the Museum of Garden History.*

SCYTHES
Solid Crown 24in. 20/3 30in. 20/3
36in. 21/3
Rivetted 30in. 13/9 36in. 14/3

SCYTHE STONES
Sandstone, square or round tapered 1/3
Carborundum 198 flat tapered 1/9
Carborundum 191c oval 2/3
Carborundum 203 round tapered 3/3

Wooden Hay Rakes 17 teeth Long handle 6/- each
Hay Forks Strapped 16/- each

REAP HOOKS
Fussell's cranked Reap Hook with crutch handle.
No. 2 (each) 12/-
Reap Hook, lighter quality No. 0 6/-, No. 1 6/6, No. 2 6/9
Light Grass Hook with detachable blade (each) 5/3
Spare Blades (each) 3/3

SNEATHS
American ring pattern (each) 22/6
Hooks (each) 7d.
Wedges (each) 5d.

ASTOR MULTI-SHEARS
This tool has four cutters, which operate with both the opening and closing movement of the handles. Saves time on hedge clipping, and leaves a better finish.
(per pair) 30/-

SHEARS

		BLADES	
SKELTON'S FAMOUS SHEARS			
Best Quality Plain Shears	... ...	7in.	14/6
Best Quality Plain Shears	... ...	8in.	16/6
Best Quality Notched Shears	... ...	9in.	19/-
Heeley's Plain Shears (Cemetery)	...	6in.	7/-
Heeley's Plain Shears (light)	... ...	8in.	10/-
Medium Quality Notched Shears	...	9in.	15/6
Border Shears—Ladies'	... ...	7in.	30/-
Border Shears—Gents'	... ...	9in.	33/-
Lawn Shears—Ladies'	... ...	7in.	30/-
Lawn Shears—Gents'	... ...	9in.	33/-
WILKINSON'S SWORD STEEL SHEARS			
Ladies' (light)	... ...	7in.	27/-
Garden Shears (Plain)	... ...	8in.	35/-
Hedging Shears (Notched)	... ...	8in.	37/-
Improved Garden Shears (with five new features as advertised)		8in.	30/-
Border Shears (Tubular Steel Handles)	...	8in.	50/-
Lawn Shears (Tubular Steel Handles)	...	8in.	60/-
SPRING SHEARS			
Spring Grass Shears (Plain)	... ...	6in.	9/-
Spring Grass Shears (Cranked)	...	6½in.	12/-
Imperfect Sheep Shears (assorted)	...		5/-

Detail.

Topiary forms, 20th century, American. *Courtesy of Larkspur Farms.*

An Astor type shears, c. 1920, English.

Topiary form, 20th century, American. *Courtesy of Larkspur Farms.*

Topiary form, 20th century, American. *Courtesy of Larkspur Farms.*

Topiary form, Victorian. *Courtesy of Riverbank Antiques.*

Topiary form, 20th century, American

Topiary forms, Victorian, English, $35-60. *Courtesy of Riverbank Antiques.*

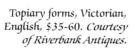

145

20th century topiary form, American. *Courtesy of Riverbank Antiques.*

Long-handled weed whacker, 19th century-early 20th century, American, $35-50. *Courtesy of The Sugarplum.*

An early version of a weed whacker, 20th century, English, c. 1920, $35-40. *Courtesy of Riverbank Antiques.*

Topiary bird form, American, 20th century. *Courtesy of Riverbank Antiques.*

9

Lawns

Lawn mowers

Lawns have always been the most visible clue as to whether or not a home or an estate has been well maintained, but keeping a lawn well mowed has not always been easy. Before the lawn-mowing machine was invented in the 1800s, estate owners and gardeners had to rely on grazing flocks of sheep, or workers with hand-held scythes.

The first patent for a lawn mowing machine was recorded in 1830 by an Englishman, Edwin Beard Budding. This was a revolution for the gardener and freed him from what had been a tiresome and arduous labor.

Scythes gave way to lawn mowers in the second half of the nineteenth century. Budding's invention had been greeted with enthusiasm by everyone. His and subsequent machines were noteworthy for their inventiveness, ingenuity, and relative ease of operation. In 1850 Thomas Green of Leeds produced another version, a gear driven mower. By the 1870s, "horse-drawn" mowers were in general use. In 1880 Ransome advertised a "horse powered" lawn mower as well as a "pony driven" lawn mower. An 1880 advertisement for a Ransome's lawn mower promised that the "horse power" lawn mower will have a "grass box, adjustable handles, a wind guard to prevent the grass from blowing about, and automatic gears." It also came with an attachment for the horse and a seat for the gardener. In its advertisement for an 1893 team mower, the company promised that their machines were "suitable for mowing gorse," a plant indigenous to England and Scotland.

In 1895 popular manufacturers Ransome, ATCO, and Green introduced steam driven mowers. In 1902 Ransome was making gas-powered lawn mowers.

Photo by Monika Dorman.

Lawns have always been the most visible clue as to whether or not a home or an estate has been well maintained, but keeping a lawn well mowed has not always been easy. Before lawn mowers were invented, gardeners had to rely on grazing flocks of sheep, or workers with scythes or sickles.

Detail.

Early 20th century lawn mower, English. *Courtesy of the Museum of Garden History.*

Detail.

Closer view.

Pony and Horse Boots

A smooth lawn was the ultimate goal of all estate owners who maintained large staffs to mow, roll and manicure their lawns. And although the new horse-drawn machines did little damage to lawns, the shod feet of the horses or ponies pulling the mowers tore up the turf, particularly as both machines and horses got larger. In the 1890s manufacturers developed a series of horse boots to be strapped on the horse's feet. Originally these boots were made by local saddlers. Eventually they were mass-produced in standard sizes.

Sickle, 19th-20th century, English. *Courtesy of the Museum of Garden History.*

Sickle, American, c. 1900, $40-60. *Courtesy of The Sugarplum.*

A decorative, painted, long-handled scythe, late 19th –early 20th century, French. *Courtesy of Riverbank Antiques.*

Detail of above.

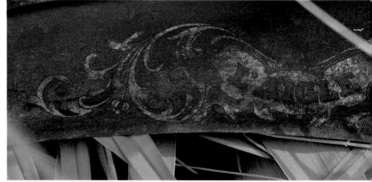

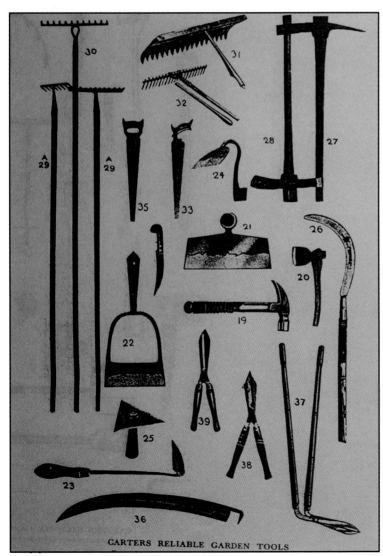

Long-handled scythes, 20th century, American, $45-60. *Courtesy of Larkspur Farms*

CARTERS RELIABLE GARDEN TOOLS

A page from a 1931 Carters garden catalog, English.

Vintage postcard, English, c. 1900, showing English gardeners pulling an early rotary lawn mower with a pony booted clad horse. Note the other gardener with his pruning clippers. It is very rare to find a good photograph of a horse wearing its pony boots. This card would be worth $25-35. *Courtesy of the Museum of Garden History.*

Kneepads, or knee protectors, English, late 19th century. These pads were used to save the knees when weeding. They also protected the gardener's pants since buying new work clothes was an expensive luxury. *Courtesy of the Museum of Garden History.*

Detail. Note the primitive nature of this early mower and, check the horse's feet. Pony boots came in two sizes. This is obviously the larger size. *Courtesy of the Museum of Garden History.*

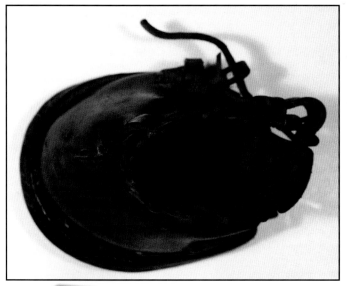

Smaller sized pony boots, early 20th century, English. Used to protect the lawn when the pony/horse was pulling a rotary lawnmower. *Courtesy of the Museum of Garden History.*

Large sized pony boot, early 20th century, English. These were used to protect the lawns when the horse was pulling a lawn mower. *Courtesy of the Museum of Garden History.*

Bottom left: Tree climbing stirrups, early 20th century, English. You put your feet in the stirrups, with the spike facing inwards and the pad is placed against the leg. Originally there were straps through the top holes to tie them to the leg. Since boots were expensive for the average working man, many garden tools had lifts to protect the boots. Garden stirrups were intended to protect boots from daily digging. *Courtesy of the Museum of Garden History.*

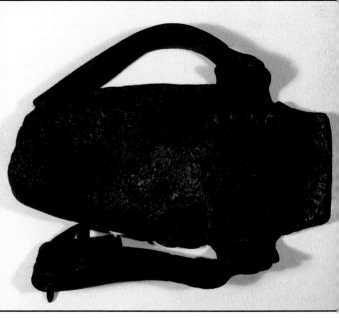

Another form of knee protectors or kneepads, English, 19th century. *Courtesy of the Museum of Garden History.*

Vintage postcard, Edwardian, $5-10, English. *Courtesy of the Museum of Garden History.*

This popular stage star posed for the press with her lawn mower. *Courtesy of the Museum of Garden History.*

Vintage Edwardian postcard. It took two men to pull this early mower. *Courtesy of the Museum of Garden History.*

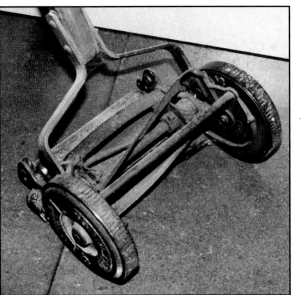

Lawn mower, Whirlwind Luton Lawnmower. Marked "made in USA." 10" blades, c. 1930. *Courtesy of the Museum of Garden History.*

Another view.

Tennis line painter, inscribed No. 2 improved Cavendish White Line Painter made by P.H. Ayres London, c. 1910. Used to mark white lines on grass tennis courts. *Courtesy of the Museum of Garden History.*

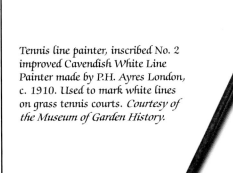

Vintage postcard, Victorian, English $10-12. *Courtesy of the Museum of Garden History.*

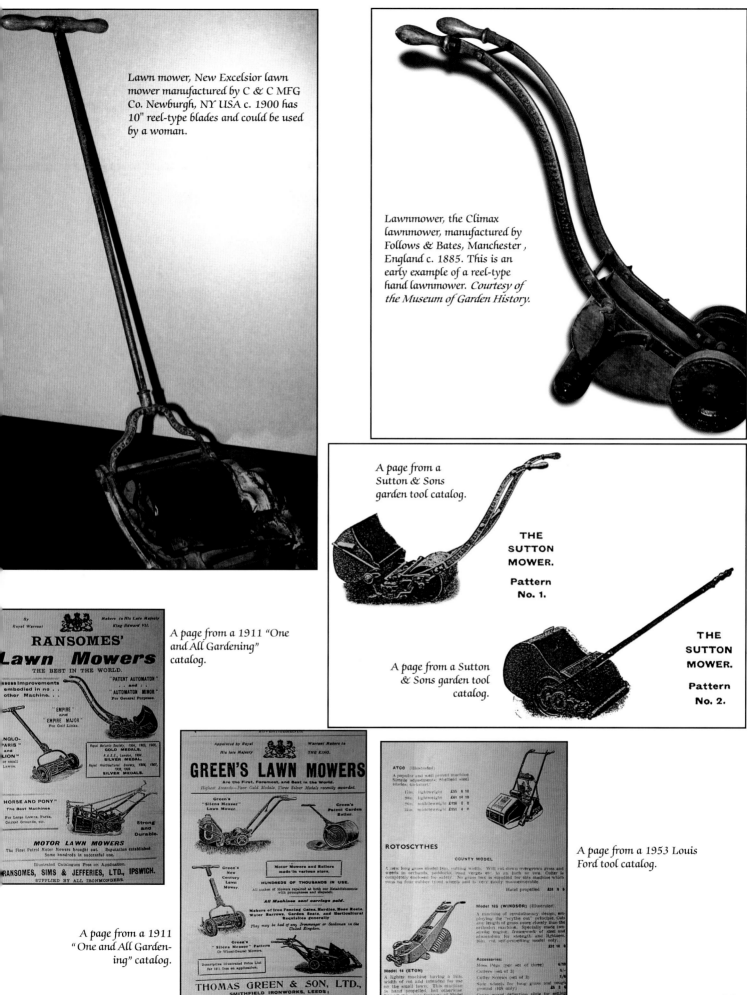

Lawn mower, New Excelsior lawn mower manufactured by C & C MFG Co. Newburgh, NY USA c. 1900 has 10" reel-type blades and could be used by a woman.

Lawnmower, the Climax lawnmower, manufactured by Follows & Bates, Manchester, England c. 1885. This is an early example of a reel-type hand lawnmower. *Courtesy of the Museum of Garden History.*

A page from a Sutton & Sons garden tool catalog.

THE SUTTON MOWER. Pattern No. 1.

A page from a Sutton & Sons garden tool catalog.

THE SUTTON MOWER. Pattern No. 2.

A page from a 1911 "One and All Gardening" catalog.

A page from a 1911 "One and All Gardening" catalog.

A page from a 1953 Louis Ford tool catalog.

Child's lawn mower.

Detail

Child's lawnmower, c. 1900, English,
$150-180. *Courtesy of The Sugarplum.*

Vintage Edwardian postcard.
*Courtesy of the Museum of
Garden History.*

Vintage postcard.
*Courtesy of the Museum
of Garden History.*

Lawn roller or leveler, English, c. 1900, $150.
Courtesy of The Sugarplum.

Tool catalog, 20ᵗʰ century,
American.

Child's lawn roller, 20ᵗʰ century, English, $125-130.

Detail

157

Lawn Rollers

The first recorded roller was marble and was dated 1259. Other variations were made of wood and stone. But these early rollers tended to produce irregular surfaces. It wasn't until the invention of the cast iron roller in the late eighteenth century that gardeners could achieve their ultimate dream- a perfect lawn surface.

Lawn mowers and lawn rollers are priced according to size, condition, historical significance and quality of design. Early lawn mowers had elaborate designs, (some even had lion shields,) and turned wooden handles. Prices range from $75-$150.

Lawn Toys and Children's Games

Gardening has always been a family activity. By the early nineteenth century horticultural societies were encouraging families to grow flower and vegetable gardens and children were encouraged to help their parents, particularly their fathers, learn to identify flowers and plants.

The Victorians loved nature and often gave their children miniature, child-sized garden tools. Parents thought that gardening was educational and taught children about nature. It also taught diligence and character. In the twentieth century, toy companies were producing die-cast garden tools.

Botany books for children have been found dating back to the 1800s. One of the earliest was *Anonymous Botanique de la Jeunesse* which was published in Paris in 1812 and is now valued at $750 plus. In 1842 Mary Tyler Mann, the wife of American educator Horace Mann, wrote a book, *A Lady: The Flower People*, an illustrated story for children. Today the book is valued at $350. In 1855 Jane Loudon wrote an illustrated book on botany and gardening for children, *My Own Garden: Or, The Young Gardener's Year Book* which provides instructions for young children on gardening activities with separate instructions for each of the four seasons. It sells for $250 plus. In the 1900s Gertrude Jekyll wrote books on gardening for children.

Home entertainments revolved around the garden, and physical games like croquet and lawn bowling became very popular. Today Victorian see-saws, lawn bowling sets, and croquet mallets and balls have become highly collectible. In good condition they are valued between $85-$150. Complete sets of Edwardian croquet balls and mallets command higher prices.

Prices are effected by quality of detail and if there is a lot of color on the original box. Victorian and Edwardian period games are very collectible, very desirable and extremely rare. Prices range from $75-$150.

19th century, American croquet mallets, $65-75. *Courtesy of Riverbank Antiques.*

Child's see-saw, Victorian, American, late 19th century, $125-150. *Courtesy of Riverbank Antiques.*

Child's scooter, c. 1900, American, $100-125. *Courtesy of Riverbank Antiques.*

Lawn bowling balls, 19th century-20th century, American, $75-85. *Courtesy of Riverbank Antiques.*

Boot Scrapers

Boot scrapers have become an interesting collectible. The Victorians, in particular, favored ornate cast iron decorative scrapers with a tray. Later garden manufacturers made a one-piece boot scraper. These cast iron scrapers were placed near the garden to keep working boots clean of clay, dirt, and mud. It is interesting to note that in the eighteenth century while watering crops, many French gardeners worked barefoot in the fields to protect their shoes and boots from water rot and other damage.

Photo by Monika Dorman.

Bootscraper, 20th century. *Courtesy of AfterMath Acres.*

Bootscraper, 19ᵗʰ century, cast iron. *Courtesy of Barbara Israel Garden Antiques.*

Bootscrapers were either very ornate in design or simple like this utilitarian one. *Courtesy of Barbara Israel Garden Antiques.*

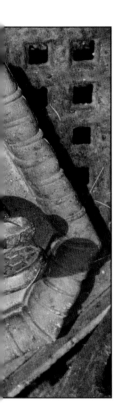

A more ornate bootscraper. *Courtesy of Barbara Israel Garden Antiques.*

Bootscraper, 19th century, cast iron, $65 . *Courtesy of Riverbank Antiques.*

Victorian bootscraper. *Courtesy of Riverbank Antiques.*

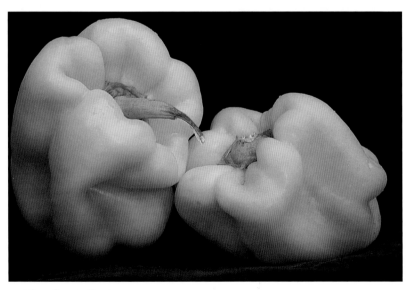

Photo by Monika Dorman.

Some bootscrapers were bolted into place.
Courtesy of Riverbank Antiques.

Bootscraper, Victorian, cast iron,
American/English.

Bootscraper, Victorian cast iron. Note
the two dolphins. Dolphins were a
popular motif in garden ornaments.

10

Harvesting, Gathering, and Carrying

Fruit Pickers & Ladders

One of the most essential parts of the gardening process is the gathering and harvesting of the fruits of labor. This process requires the most hands-on supervision in the sorting and processing of the harvest.

The earliest French fruit pickers date from 1780 and were called "pomettes" or "little apples." These early hand-held fruit pickers were made of rattan, wood, wire or tin and were attached to long wooden poles. Most of these pickers were shaped like a pocket or a glove mitt. Often rope baskets were also attached to these pickers to catch the fruit.

Advertisers noted that long-poled fruit pickers were safer and more convenient than ladders.

An interesting specific adaptation of a fruit picking basket is the "apple picking bag," a reinforced canvas/leather bag that would hang from the worker's shoulder. The bottom of this basket was secured with a drawstring which, when released, allowed the apples to drop into a bin.

Fruit picking ladders are usually triangular and tapered at the top so that when they are placed against a tree or moved around in the orchard their rungs will not interfere with or damage the fruit laden branches.

Ladders range in price from $175-$250. Apple picking bags range in price from $75 to $90 depending on condition.

Photo by Monika Dorman.

Wheelbarrows

From early history man has been inventing tools to help make his labors easier. The invention of the wheel elevated man from being a beast of burden and enabled him to create a vehicle he could push or pull with a minimum of effort. Wheelbarrows have been in use since the Middle Ages when a "barrow" was invented to carry produce. Until the nineteenth century most wheelbarrows were made of wood. In the nineteenth century, wheelbarrows were first manufactured in wrought iron. Since then wheelbarrows have been ubiquitous in fields, gardens, and at home, and have transported food, produce, grass, and hay.

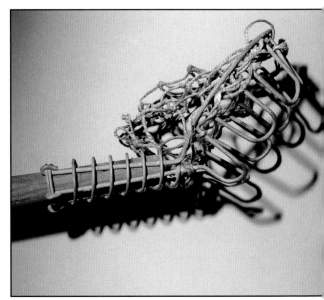

Fruit picker, 19th century. *Courtesy of the Museum of Garden History.*

Apple picker, 20th century, American. *Courtesy of Riverbank Antiques.*

Fruit picker, tin, Victorian. Usually only the heads of the fruit pickers survived and the poles had to be replaced. *Courtesy of Riverbank Antiques.*

Detail

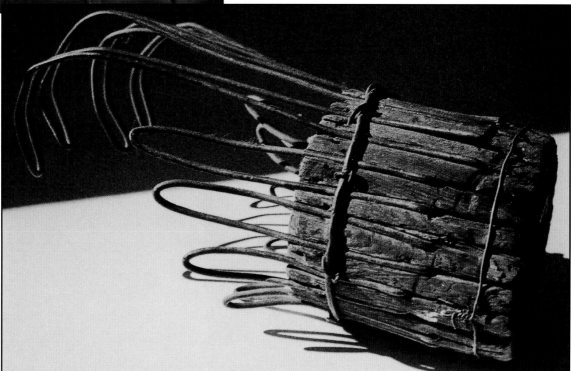

Fruit picker, 20th century, American, a Florida citrus fruit picker.

The "Ideal" Fruit Gatherer.

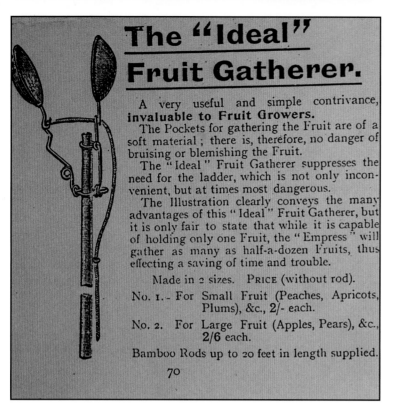

A very useful and simple contrivance, **invaluable to Fruit Growers.**

The Pockets for gathering the Fruit are of a soft material; there is, therefore, no danger of bruising or blemishing the Fruit.

The "Ideal" Fruit Gatherer suppresses the need for the ladder, which is not only inconvenient, but at times most dangerous.

The Illustration clearly conveys the many advantages of this "Ideal" Fruit Gatherer, but it is only fair to state that while it is capable of holding only one Fruit, the "Empress" will gather as many as half-a-dozen Fruits, thus effecting a saving of time and trouble.

Made in 2 sizes.   PRICE (without rod).

No. 1.—For Small Fruit (Peaches, Apricots, Plums), &c., 2/- each.

No. 2. For Large Fruit (Apples, Pears), &c., 2/6 each.

Bamboo Rods up to 20 feet in length supplied.

70

A page from a 1909 Wood & Son garden tool catalog. Hand held fruit pickers were advertised as being safer and more convenient than ladders for picking fruit. Wood & Son advertised that a good fruit picker would pay for itself in a week by picking but not damaging ripe fruit.

The "Birdsall"

Combined Flower Gatherer and Holder.

The Blades of Best Sheffield Steel. Highly finished Brass Joints, fitted with Strong Bamboo Cane Handle to any length not exceeding 20 feet.

24/- each.

A page from a 1909 Wood & Son garden tool catalog.

The "Empress" Fruit Gatherer

Will save its cost in a week.

A perfect boon to the Grower.

The bag is made of Rot-proof material, and a hood is formed which prevents any possibility of the fruit falling outside. A simple opening is arranged at the bottom by which it is speedily emptied.

6 ft., 7/6; 8 ft., 8/6; 10 ft., 9/6; 12 ft., 10/6.

166

A page from a 1909 Wood & Son garden tool catalog.

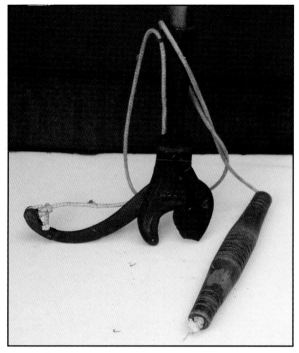

Detail

Apple pickers basket, c. 1943, French, $125-150. *Courtesy of Riverbank Antiques.*

Fruit picker, 19th century, American, $45-50. *Courtesy of Riverbank Antiques.*

Wheelbarrow, American, 20th century. *Courtesy of the White Swan Guest House.*

Child's wheel barrow, 20th century American. *Courtesy of Larkspur Farms.*

Garden Flag, 20ᵗʰ century American. Garden flags have all kinds of floral and garden motifs. They have become an increasingly popular collectible within the last fifteen years. This one has a charming wheel barrow design.

Vintage postcard, 1920s, English, $5-8.
Courtesy of the Museum of Garden History.

Wood was the traditional material for barrows. Today it is more common to find wheelbarrows made out of galvanized metal or aluminum.

Child's sized wheelbarrow, 20th century. *Courtesy of Larkspur Farms.*

Wheelbarrow, 19th century, French, wood. *Courtesy of Riverbank Antiques.*

Wheelbarrow, 19th century, French. *Courtesy of Riverbank Antiques.*

Child's wheelbarrow, Edwardian, English. *Courtesy of the Museum of Garden History.* The family's chauffeur made this wheelbarrow for Master Griffiths

Child's wheelbarrows.

Wheelbarrow, 19th-20th century, Brazilian.

Vintage postcard, Edwardian, English, $5-8. *Courtesy of the Museum of Garden History.*

Close up detail. Usually only the basket heads survived and the poles had to be replaced.

Wheel barrow, 20th century, American.

Westchester, New York.

Apple picking ladder, 19th century, French, $175-250. *Courtesy of The Sugarplum.*

Wooden handbarrow, 19th century, English. *Courtesy of the Museum of Garden History.*

Hand barrow, 19th century, English. *Courtesy of the Museum of Garden History.*

Apple picking ladder.

Apple picking ladder.

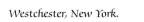

Fruit picking basket/cane, 20th century, English. *Courtesy of the Museum of Garden History.*

Photo by Monika Dorman.

171

Harvest Baskets, Fruit Baskets, Grocers' Baskets, Sifters, Winnowing Dishes, Drying Racks, & Trugs

Lightweight, portable containers have been made out of straw, rattan, reeds, bamboo and grass for thousands of years. Easy to carry and stack, these baskets have been carried by hand, hung on shoulders, and balanced on heads. Grocers' baskets, wine baskets, winnowing and sifting baskets, and seed baskets range in value from $85-$350 depending on design, condition and origin.

Storage baskets usually have reinforced edges so that they can support the weight of other stacked baskets. Grape baskets are usually marked with the vineyard or owners' initials. Many of the larger baskets have grips on each end so that they can be carried easily by one or two men.

From 1890-1930 the English used wooden slatted baskets with wooden rudder bottoms called "trugs." These baskets are usually valued at $85-$150 according to size.

Fruit, such as plums or grapes were placed on long triangular drying racks or sorting baskets, left in dark, cool rooms, to dry. Sorting baskets and sorting racks had removable bottoms, or perforated trays that gauged the size of bulbs, fruits and onions. The trays came with different sized holes to measure the fruit. Bulb winnowing or sifting dishes also had interchangeable bottoms to sift and measure the bulbs. They also sifted the dirt off the harvested bulbs.

Vintage postcard, Edwardian, $5-10. *Courtesy of the Museum of Garden History.*

Photo by Monika Dorman.

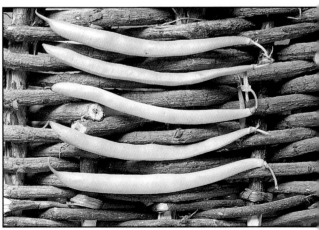

Photo by Monika Dorman.

Photo by Monika Dorman.

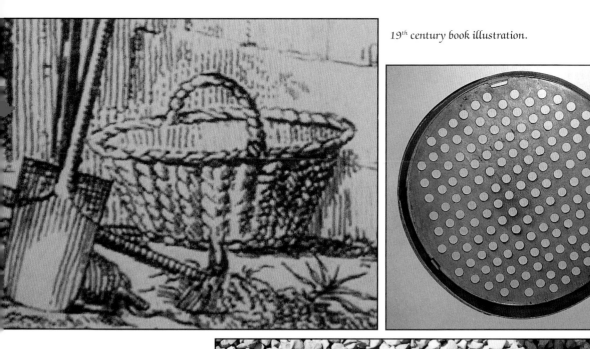
19th century book illustration.

Detail of a winnowing basket. Each came with removable inside lids. Each had different sized holes.

Basket, 20th century, English, $65. *Courtesy of the Museum of Garden History.*

CHARLES & CO. GROCERS AND FRUITERERS NEW YORK

Detail.

Grocer's basket, 20th century, American, $100-150. *Courtesy of Riverbank Antiques.*

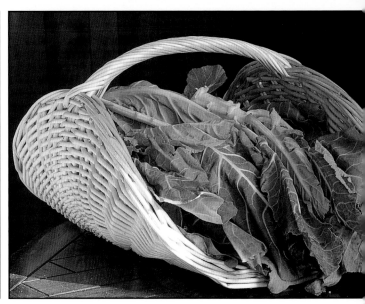

Assorted fruit gathering baskets, 19th century French and English. *Courtesy of Riverbank Antiques.*

French grape growers basket, $200-250. *Courtesy of Riverbank Antiques.*

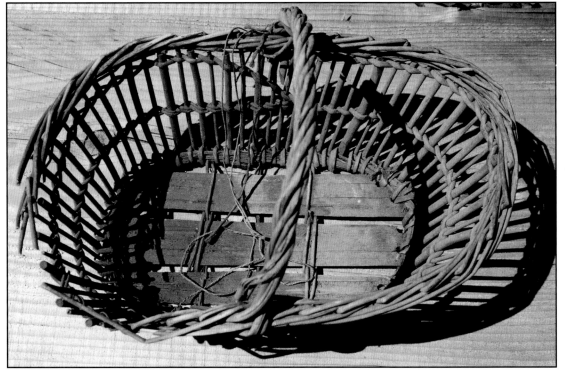

Basket, 19th century, English, $65-80. *Courtesy of Riverbank Antiques.*

Photo by Monika Dorman.

A page from a 1926 Carters catalog

Trug, c. 1900, English, $50-200. These wooden baskets were called trugs and made in England from 1890-1930. *Courtesy of The Sugarplum.*

Another version of an English trug.

English, 19th-20th century. Trugs are valued at $100-200 depending on condition and size. These baskets have also been called melon baskets because they resemble a half melon. *Courtesy of The Sugarplum.*

A walking stick basket , 1980, English. Devised for elderly apple/pear pickers. *Courtesy of the Museum of Garden History.*

Fruit drying screens, 19th century French. Probably used for fruits such as plums. *Courtesy of Riverbank Antiques.*

This 20th century English walking basket was originally a grocer's basket, but eventually gardeners saw its usefulness and wheeled it into their gardens.

Bulb sifting basket, English, c. 1900, $60-85. Baskets like these came with removable insides with varying sized holes, and were used to sift and measure the bulbs. This basket also sifted the dirt off the bulbs. *Courtesy of Riverbank Antiques.*

Grape Pickers, Baskets, & Savers

All tools relating to the grape harvest are French in origin, since the French were more interested in gastronomy and food harvest than the English. French gardeners were particularly interested in wine and the development of their vineyards. So it is safe to assume that all tools that have to do with grape cultivation are usually French in origin.

In the late nineteenth century, the French used short, squat glass bottles to preserve their grapes. The French placed the stems of the bunches of grapes in water in these bottles and stored them on angled shelves in dark, cool rooms so that the grapes could be eaten months later. Later the English designed a novelty grape-preserving bottle, a long narrow bottle with an angled neck. The most common version was a Copped Hall made by Wood & Son during the years 1910-1930.

Photo by Monika Dorman.

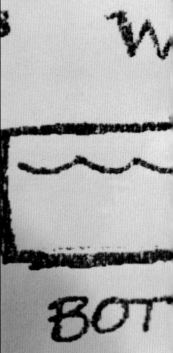

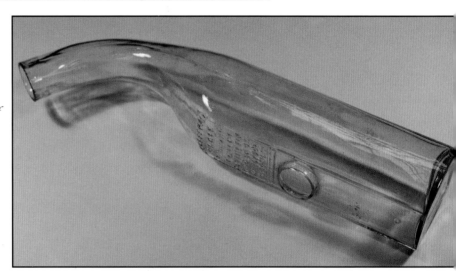

Grape preserver bottle, English,
19th century. *Courtesy of
Riverbank Antiques.*

This grape storage bottle was manufactured both as
practical item and as a novelty. The most common version
was this Copped Hall patent made by Wood & Son. A
section of vine with a clump of grapes was placed in water
in the bottle and stored in a cool, dark place to be eaten
later c. 1910-1930.

178

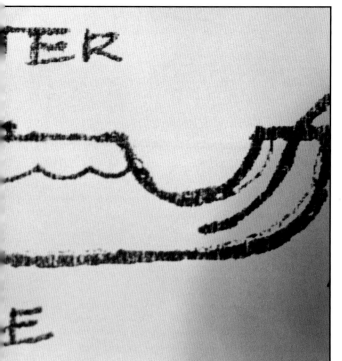

The grape stem was placed in the neck of the bottle and the bottle was then filled with water. *Drawing by Philip Norman.*

Grape preserving bottles, French and English, 19th-20th century. The French used short squat bottles to store the grapes. The English invented their own variation, a tall, slender bottle with an elongated neck.

11

Displays

Flower Frogs

Flower frogs are flower holders with multiple holes on wire baskets to hold individual stems in a pleasing display. While we have found several wonderful ceramic and porcelain versions from the eighteenth and early nineteenth centuries, the most popular Victorian era style are "free-form sculptural wire stands." In the twentieth century flower frogs became more functional and were usually rigid forms with sharp projections. Ordinary flower frogs are valued at $20-$35. More intricate and sculptural forms can be valued at upwards of $85.

Photo by Monika Dorman.

A ceramic pond frog. *Courtesy of Riverbank Antiques.*

Flower frog, American, early 20th century, concrete.

Vintage flower frog, 20th century, American.

Flower frogs, Japanese, c. 1890-1920, $65-75 each. *Courtesy of Riverbank Antiques.*

Flower frog, Wedgwood crocus pot in the shape of an armadillo, with an under tray, c. 1840. *Courtesy of Riverbank Antiques.*

Flower frog, crocus pot, lacks base, c. 1840, English. *Courtesy of Riverbank Antiques.*

Flower frog, origin unknown, 19th century.

Flower frog, c. 1920, Japanese, $65-75. *Courtesy of Riverbank Antiques.*

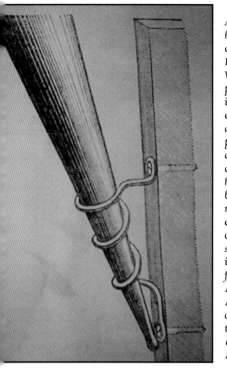

A bracket tube holder, 19th century, glass, English. The Victorians were particularly interested in exhibiting and displaying their prized specimens and flowers, and contemporary horticultural books and magazines extensively covered the subject. This illustration is from the *Horticultural Exhibitor*, a 19th century, English trade journal. *Courtesy of Hinck and Wall.*

Flower frogs, early 20th century, American, $20-35.

Flower frog, English, c. 1920, $40-75.

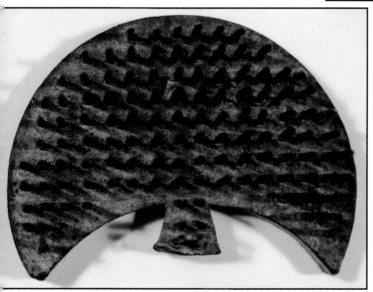

Flower frog, c. 1950, American, $15-20. *Courtesy of Riverbank Antiques.*

Vintage flower frog, early 20th century. It is very unusual to find a flower frog that is rounded in the bottom so that it fits into a flowerpot. *Courtesy of the Sugarplum.*

183

Flower frog, c. 1920, English, $50-85.

Flower frogs, 20th century, English. $25-45. *Courtesy of Riverbank Antiques.*

Flower frog, early 20th century. *Courtesy of the Sugarplum.*

Another version.

Flower frogs, $40-65.

Flower frog, English, $40-75.

Flower frogs, Victorian, English, $45-75. Victorian wire flower frogs are valued upwards of $75 depending on intricacy and condition. Many of them are highly regarded for their sculptural design. *Courtesy of Riverbank Antiques.*

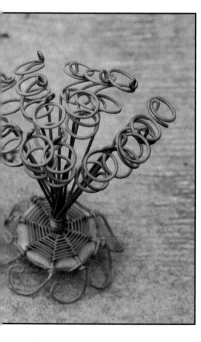

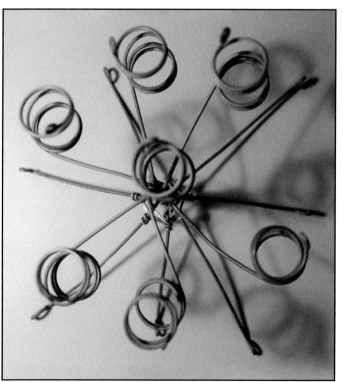

Flower frog, English, c. 1920, $30-50.

Victorian flower frog, English, $40-75.

Flower frog, Victorian, English.

Flower frog, Victorian.

Florist Buckets & Display Stands

Victorian florists used a variety of metal flower stands. Today they are very collectible. During Victorian days and throughout the early twentieth century, hostesses liked to arrange freshly picked flowers.

These Victorian floral stands range in price from $75-$150 depending on condition, age, design, and detail.

Florist display buckets, red enamel, 20th century, $35-40. *Courtesy of Larkspur Farms.*

Watering pails, 20th century, American. *Courtesy of Larkspur Farms.*

Photo by Monika Dorman.

Florist display stand, 19th century-early 20th century, English, $135-165. *Courtesy of Riverbank Antiques.*

Florist display holder, French, c. 1920-1930, zinc $200-250. *Courtesy of Riverbank Antiques.*

Galvanized water pail, 20th century, American.

Detail.

Container from the Royal Horticultural Society. $65-75. *Courtesy of Riverbank Antiques.*

Florist display buckets, English, c. 1900, $50-125. *Courtesy of Riverbank Antiques.*

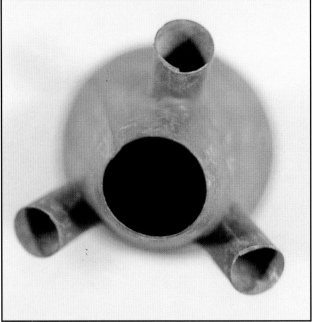

Tin flower frog, English, c. 1900, $50-125. This is a very rare flower frog both because of its size and its shape. *Courtesy of The Sugarplum.*

12

Miscellaneous

Photo by Monika Dorman.

Awards

Beginning in the early nineteenth century horticultural societies sprung up in Europe and in the United States and soon these gardening groups were rewarding their members' efforts with awards and trophies. Gardeners began to raise unusual specimens and by the mid-nineteenth century, there were gardening competitions. Most of the medals and awards in this book date from the mid-1800s through the mid-1900s. In Britain the most coveted gardening awards are those of Royal Horticultural Society.

A mold for a weathervane.

It is difficult to price these awards. Pricing depends on materials, whether the award is sterling silver, brass, copper etc., age, condition and prestige of the institution or the person receiving the award. Generally pricing ranges from $50-$175.

The following medals and awards are from the collection of the Museum of Garden History.

School Horticultural Championship Medal inscribed "Presented by Toogood and Sons LTD. Southampton , Seedsmen to HM The King," bronze, c. 1910.

Medal, c. 1850, silver gilt. "Loyal and Independent Gardeners" and "Let Brotherly Love Continue" written on side. British.

Other side.

Medal from Aberdeen Horticultural Society, 1835, silver, Scottish. Inscribed "To Mr. Robert Adams, Schoolmaster N. Banchory."

The reverse side

Reverse

Medal inscribed "E.W.M.F.S.1923 Tillie White Medal won by H.E. Fergusson." Silver , probably English, 1923.

Medal Aberdeenshire Horticultural Society, 1830, Scotland. Silver, Inscribed "Robert Adam for Hollyhocks 3 Nov. 1830."

Reverse side of Aberdeenshire Horticultural Society medal.

Gardening trophy, 20th century, English, bronze, $75-120. *Courtesy of The Sugarplum.*

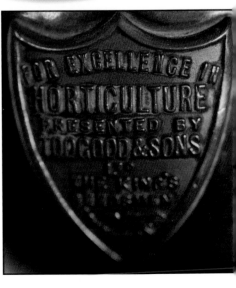

Detail.

Mechanical calendar, 20th century, $35-45.
Courtesy of The Sugarplum.

Garden angels made by California artist, Claudia
Ellis, 20th century, American, $95-$250.
Courtesy of Sallie Mac.

Garden bench, 20th century, American. *Courtesy of the
Mendocino Ceramics Studio, Mendocino, California.*

Leaf shaped metal table, 20th century, American, maker unknown. $35-60. *Courtesy of Riverbank Antiques.*

Bertoia butterfly chairs, 20th century, American, aluminum mesh, $45-85. *Courtesy of Riverbank Antiques.*

A Richard Schultz design chairs, 1966 collection. $1500-1800 each.

196

Adirondack porch chairs, wood,
20th century, American, $75-100.

California ceramic artist Jan Hinson made the
following ceramic chairs. $4000-$11,000. *Courtesy
of the Mendocino Ceramics Studio.*

One of the authors taking a pause in a Hinson chair, Mendocino Ceramics Studio.

Garden flags

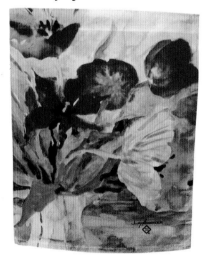

Garden flag, 1999, American.

Tools in the Garden

What stories these tools could tell! One looks at these wonderfully worn and burnished dibbers, shovels, hoes, and pruning knives. Who used them? What were their gardens like? We will never know.

The "Tradescant Window" of the Museum of Garden History, 1981, designed by Lawrence Lee.

Center right: Baskets of raspberries, LaConner, Washington.

Bottom right: *Courtesy of Gramercy Tavern. Roberta BenDavid Designs*

Rakes, 20th century, Pantanel, Brazil.

Wooden topiary forms, 20th century, American. *Courtesy of Larkspur Farms.*

Ceramic urn, 20th century, French. *Courtesy of Riverbank Antiques.*

Metal topiary form, 20th century, American.

Decorative rake head, *Courtesy of Gramercy Tavern. Roberta BenDavid Designs.*

Watering pitcher, early 20th century, American. *Courtesy of Larkspur Farms.*

Miniature garden sprayer. This was either made for a child or was a manufacturer's sample. *Courtesy of Barbara Israel Garden Antiques.*

Watering can, 20th century, galvanized metal, American.

Watering can, galvanized metal, 20th century, American. *Courtesy of the White Swan Guest House.*

Courtesy of Gramercy Tavern, Roberta Ben David Designs.

The White Swan Guest House.

13

Pricing Ranges

Pricing antique garden tools is difficult since many are still used by active gardeners. Nineteenth century garden tools were so well designed that many gardeners prize the older tools more than they do their newer replacements. We have found that tools vary in price depending on where they were bought. On the other hand, often very valuable tools are sold cheaply because they were bought by dealers as part of an estate. It is also common to find very good antique tools in baskets and bins at flea markets. Since the marketplace and availability determine pricing, in some cases in this book it might seem as if our individual prices are in conflict with our average price ranges. But in fact while we have offered pricing averages, we have also noted the prices of the objects we have found in retail shops.

The year 1850 seems to be a cut-off date for pricing tools. Pre-1850 tools have historic interest. Post-1850 tools have more collectible interest. Garden tool collections are difficult to store and most serious tool collectors have access to storage sheds, garages and warehouses. We have found that smaller pieces bring relatively higher prices than larger, more ungainly tools because the smaller pieces are more attractive to collectors who have space constraints.

The Museum of Garden History in London has an excellent collection of tools numbering more than 2000. Since the museum prizes these implements, many gardeners have donated their old tools to the museum. We have also found wonderful old tools in garden sheds rusting away.

In general, tools that are pre-1850, or have unusual shapes and functions command the highest prices. Ordinary late nineteenth and early twentieth century tools are usually valued between $35-$50. Children's tools are very collectible and are worth double the price of their adult counterparts.

Among ordinary tools, terracotta forcers are the most sought after and desirable and usually sell for $150- $400. They are quite expensive and rare because few have survived intact. Victorian cloches in general are valued at $200-$300.

Pricing garden tools is a relatively new field, and prices are more often determined by how much the dealer spent for them rather than by their intrinsic value, condition or desirability. Many American dealers make regular buying trips to England and France. Therefore we have more information about French, English, and American tools than we do about Italian,

German, and other European tools. We have had to approximate value for individual tools we couldn't find in the marketplace. Others we have left unpriced because they are part of private collections. The authors and publisher of this book do not assume any responsibility for any sales or transactions based on information gained from this book.

Photo by Monika Dorman.

Sprinkler head, 20th century, English.

Places to Visit

The Museum of Garden History
Lambeth Palace Road
London SE 1 7LB
020- 7401-8865
FAX 020-7401-8869

The Lawn Mower Museum
Trerice House, Kestle Mill, Newquay Cornwall TR 8 4PG
England
Tel. 44-1637- 875 404

The Lawn Mower Museum
107-114 Shakespeare Street
Southport, Lancashire PR8 5a

Trevano Estate and Gardens
Helston, Cornwall TR13 0RU (Tel. 01326574274)

Resources

Lynn Chase
Riverbanks Antiques
Wells Union
1775 Post Road
Route 1
P.O Box 3009
Wells, Maine 04090
207-646-6314

Anne Elizabeth Rowe
The Sugarplum
Route 4
Danbury, New Hampshire 03230
603-768-3925
Fax 603-768-3762

Botanical Books
Hinck and Wall
P.O.Box 32266
Washington, D.C. 20007
202-965-3785

Barbara Israel Garden Antiques
Katonah, New York
1-212-744-6281

The White Swan Guest House
15872 Moore Road
Mount Vernon, Washington 98273
360-445-6805

After Math Acres
Moore Road
Mount Vernon, Washington 98273

Larkspur Farm
LaConner, Washington 98273

Tillinghast Florist and Nursery
Arberta Lammers
623 Morris St.
P.O. Box 738
LaConner, WA 98257
360-466-3329
1-800-320-3329
FAX. 360-466-1401

Gramercy Tavern
42 E. 20th Street
New York City, New York
212-477-0777

Roberta Ben David Design, Inc.
New York City, New York
212-677-7348

Haws Watering Cans
Beakes Road, Smethwick, Warley,
West Midlands, B 67 5AB, England

Garden Artists

Sallie Mac
10540 Lansing Street
Mendocino, California 95460
707-937-5357

Jan Hinson
Albion, California
707-937- 0404

Leslie Campbell
Mendocino Ceramics Studio
10551 Kastin Street
Mendocino, California 95460
707-937-3459

Mary Taylor
Rosebar
LaConner, Washington 98273

Books

Israel, Barbara. *Antique Garden Ornament: Two Centuries of American Taste.*
    New York: Harry Abrams, Inc., 1999
Morris, Alastair. *Antiques from the Garden.* England: Garden Art Press, 1999
Outwater, Myra Yellin, and Eric Boe Outwater *Garden Antiques and Ornaments.*
    Atglen, PA: Schiffer Publishing, 2000.
Outwater, Myra Yellin, and Eric Boe Outwater. *Floridiana: Collecting Florida's
    Best.* Atglen, PA: Schiffer Publishing, 1999.
Slesin, Suzanne, et al. *Everyday Things: Garden Tools.* New York: Abbeyville
    Press, 1996

Garden Prayer, 20th century, American. *Courtesy of the Range Riders Museum, Miles City, Montana.*

208